Garden of my Ancestors

Garden of my Ancestors

BRIDGET HILTON-BARBER

First published by Penguin Books (South Africa) Pty Ltd 2007
Reprinted by Penguin Books (South Africa) Pty Ltd 2008
Reprinted by Penguin Books (South Africa) Pty Ltd 2010

Reprinted by Footprints Press, South Africa 2018

Website: www.hiltonbarber.co.za

Copyright © Bridget Hilton-Barber 2018

Cover design by Anthony Cuerden
Email: ant@flyingant.co.za

Printed by Pinetown Printers (Pty) Ltd

IBSN 978-0-63993264-4

In spring for sheer delight
I set the lanterns swinging through the trees,
Bright as the myriad argosies of the night,
That ride the clouded billows of the sky,
Red dragons leap and plunge in gold and silver seas,
And O my garden gleaming cold and white,
Thou hast outshone the far faint moon on high.

Yuan Mei
From *Great Gardens of the World* by Ronald King

To the ancestors

Chapter one

A monkey skull, a black mamba; a flash of precognition, lightning. Although I've never quite got used to them, I've become more in tune with messages from my ancestors. They're a feisty lot, their methods have been dramatic. My grandmother, for example, once tried to take out one of my boyfriends with a lightning strike, while my grandfather on my father's side famously prevented a wedding from taking place by causing a flash flood in the middle of winter. My dear great-aunt, bless her heart, made a red rose flower in my garden on the loneliest Valentine's Day of my life.

Some of my friends and family have regarded these portents and omens as mere coincidence, others have dismissed them outright. Most arch a quizzical eyebrow or roll baleful eyes heavenward. What does a white gal know about that kind of stuff? But I have spent too long interacting with the ancestors now to doubt their power. Our ancestors don't die if they live in our dreams, they say in Sotho. *Badimo barena ba ka se hwe ge ba phela ditorong tsa rena.* They don't die, they just change.

That particular Wednesday morning, the ancestors sent me a strange warning. In the spirit of making a good girlfriend, Nantie, feel like a princess, I'd offered to host a dinner party that evening for her birthday and was making a chicken curry. It was a delicious offering, I was thinking, flavoured with cashew nuts, coconut milk and lemon grass, when my nose suddenly got itchy – you know that sudden maddening itch? – so I scratched it and as I looked down quickly at my hand I noticed that my lifeline had got longer.

I smeared the layer of spice mixture off my palm to make sure. It was extraordinary. Overnight, perhaps even at dawn, my lifeline had extended by a few millimetres towards my index finger. I was of course instantly grateful – who doesn't want to live longer? – but, I hate to say it, since it sounds so stupid now, I didn't stop to consider it more carefully because I was too engaged in the play of possibilities between cumin and coriander.

By the time evening fell and the thrum of distant highway traffic faded, the house was infused with the reassuring smell of home cooking and the promise of good cheer. On a restaurant style blackboard, I'd written up the birthday menu: Sweet & Spicy Butternut Soup, to be followed by the Afro-Coco Chicken Curry and, finally, coffee and a sumptuous silky chocolate cake which I'd weakly dubbed Brown Belt Chocolate Chop since the birthday girl had a black belt in karate.

I'd decorated the dining room table with garishly festive flair. A single strelitzia in a glass vase and two plastic chickens formed the centrepiece, around which twelve places had been set and fresh rose petals scattered. I'd strung pink streamers and yellow balloons from the curtain rod, along with the *pièce de résistance* of bistro kitsch – a string of flashing electric plastic grapes.

I think I last checked the kitchen clock at around 7pm and decided that such a good hostess deserved a generous glass of wine. So I poured an enormous glass of Fat Bastard Chardonnay and went and lay down on the lounge floor next to the heater and the cat. I remember the Soweto String Quartet was playing a *Sarie Marais* medley, of all things – the refrain goes: *Hier kom die Ali Bama, die Ali Bama, die Ali Ba* ... – when I heard the faintest of scuffles. Momentarily I thought to myself that the driveway gate was locked – and as I looked up, I looked straight into the grotesque grin of a young man – tracksuit pants, trainers, goatee – who stepped into the lounge with a flourish and pointed a 9mm pistol straight at my head.

'Fuck you, I'll kill you,' he said quietly. 'Don't move. How many in the house?'

My Afro-Tarantino moment had come.

I felt icy quicksilver fear shoot through my body. I started to scream but strangled the sound. Two other guys, one very tall, slid menacingly into the lounge. Both had guns, no masks or gloves. I started panting like a dog. Oh fuck, we're being held up, oh fuck, this is what it's like. I heard the hideous banging of my terrified heart. I don't believe it, I don't believe it, ohmigod it's real ...

'Fuck you, I'll kill you,' said Grinning Man again. 'How many in the house?'

'Two, two,' I blurted out.

Grinning Man disappeared and the second guy pointed his gun at me and told me to roll over on the carpet with my arms spread out. 'We are hungry,' he said, I guess as some perverse way of explanation, but I misunderstood. 'There's a lovely chicken curry on the stove,' I stammered. 'Fuck you, shut up,' he said. 'I kill you, no monkey thing.'

Grinning Man returned to the lounge, his gun stuck between my husband's shoulder blades. B's hands were in the air, he was saucer-eyed, ghostly, ghastly white. They pushed him to the ground next to me. Next Max, our tenant, same thing, pushed on to the lounge floor at gunpoint, blind terror frozen on her face. 'Fuck you, I shoot you,' said Grinning Man, more aggressive towards her. She was like a rat facing a cobra; she couldn't take her eyes off him.

'Don't look, fuck you, I kill you,' he said and *klapped* her on the head with the butt of his pistol.

They had brought their own cable ties and started trussing us up like chickens. 'Fuck you, where's the safe?' asked Grinning Man.

'We have no safe,' I said.

'Where's the money?' he asked.

'There's fifty rand in my wallet in my handbag.'

'Fuck you, I kill you, no monkey trick.'

'Take whatever you want, guys,' said B. 'Take anything.'

They talked amongst themselves in a mixture of Zulu and *tsotsitaal*. The tall guy didn't say a word but the other two referred to each other by name – Collins and Bethlehem – and kept up their constant refrain. Fuck you, we kill you, no monkey thing, fuck you, we shoot you, no monkey trick. Bizarrely, I was tempted to correct their language. Er, Mr Armed Robbers, the expression you're after is actually monkey *business*.

Grinning Man pulled off my shoes and I thought I was going to be raped. My body was rigid with terror, my heart pounding. In my mind, I was going through one of those Police File checklists … don't panic, don't scream, do exactly as they say, don't look at them … Then he tied my legs together and I realised it was my new Nikes that he was after, a birthday present from my husband – now a trophy for his babe? I noted, of all things, that the secret socks I was wearing had *No Fear* stitched on to their elastic. They chucked blankets from the beds over our legs and backs.

'Listen guys, *ma gents*, we have to tell you we are having a dinner party,' B said, his voice thick with fear, pleading, earnest.
'Fuck, you lie, I kill you.'

'Look at the table, *ma gents*, look at our table.'

'How many?' asked Grinning Man.

'Ten.'

'OK, we wait.'

On the Richter Scale of Fear this was more than a ten. I imagined my friends walking into this twisted scene, the three of us bound and covered, three armed men in the darkness ... Hi, is anyone home? Cold gun against a warm temple, terror, panic, disbelief. I waited for the bullet, for the bang, the blood. My cat was miaowing, rubbing her face frantically against my head. Grinning Man leaned down towards her and I thought she was going to go out with a strangled cry, but instead he stood on my reading glasses that had fallen off my face, and ground them into the floor.

From the corner of the lounge, I felt a warm energy, as if someone was there. The plastic grapes were flashing, the candles flickering, the music playing. Even to a thug it was pretty obvious a dinner party was indeed about to happen. They started a rapid pillage through the house, beginning by ripping the hi-fi from the wall, putting an abrupt end to The Soweto String Quartet. They ripped out the TV, wrenched the DVD player from its socket, upturned drawers, ransacked cupboards. Their voices were becoming louder and more urgent. The tall guy was flicking the lounge lights on and off, while the other two moved around the lounge and dining room, waving their guns about as if in some badly choreographed crime ballet, barking out the same sentences. Fuck you, we shoot you, no monkey thing.

5

They had our car keys now, our cellphones, wallets, laptops. We lay on the floor, bound and blanketed, while they moved their gear out to the cars. I heard Max's car start up, but figured the driver couldn't find reverse, because he coasted backwards down the driveway. They loaded everything into my Golf, a real takeaway of a car as they say, hah! By the time you read this there won't even be a car seat left. I heard the Golf start up, rev. The front door closed.

Then it opened again, and I heard one of them come back. Oh God, I thought, back to blow our brains out. We've seen their faces, we're history. I waited for a bullet, the bang, the blood. I hoped it was going to be quick. Out of the corner of my eye I saw Grinning Man, 9mm pistol in one hand, reaching out with the other hand and removing a golden statue of a Buddha from the entrance hall shelf. Then he closed the door with a quiet click and disappeared into the darkness. My former Golf drove down the road. Silence. It was over.

Max had been tied the least tightly and managed to wriggle out of her cable tie. She cut us free with a pair of a garden clippers lying on the table. My hands had swollen to the size of oven gloves and I had no feeling in my fingers. B called 10111 and in just a few minutes the Flying Squad arrived – at the same time as the first guests, about 7.35.

'Hey,' said my friend Kim, first one in the door, 'I haven't seen you in ages.' I started babbling and hyperventilating, choking back sobs. More police arrived, and more guests, who were horrified, disbelieving, aghast and eternally grateful to have been fashionably late at this particular dinner party.

The house filled with police and friends. I felt like an actor in a snuff movie that had just got called off. I was euphoric, gabbling, shocked, leaping around full of adrenalin. The phone was ringing off the hook. My parents, B's mother, Max's lover, good friends, anxious relatives. *We love you, we love you, thank God you're alive* ... Everything was completely surreal and dreamlike. I walked into the garden to greet more guests. There was a police car in the driveway, blue light flashing.

'Hi Bridge, see you've got a new car,' my friend Kate called out. How wrong can a girl be?

The police were fantastic. They held our hands and looked into our eyes and told us they were truly sorry. They're certainly not the horrible cops I remember from the eighties. This lot was well trained, caring, professional. Our friends sat in the dining room, opening every single bottle they could lay their hands on while B, Max and I had our statements taken in different rooms. 'Some people just talk about crime at their dinner parties ...' I heard my friend Chris saying. 'No kidding,' replied Herbie. 'I knew of one where they stole the dinner as well.'

Detectives arrived, a Fingerprints Man arrived, a Trauma Counsellor arrived and introduced herself to all the guests and handed out leaflets featuring an alarming list of normal after-effects to expect after a traumatic event like this: bad dreams, intrusive memories, fear, helplessness, guilt, anger, anxiety, a dreamlike state ... Right now, however, we must eat, drink and be merry.

It was testament to our peculiarly South African tenacity that we decided to press on with the birthday dinner. The last official to leave was the Fingerprints Man who had been tinkering around the house with his little brush, and it was nearly 10pm by the time we sat down to start the Sweet & Spicy Butternut Soup. I felt like I was in a play, a twisted modern version of The Last Supper. Or was it The First Supper? Most of us were drunk or heading that way. Everyone was fired up and pulling out their best crime story. Hey, remember when we lived in Melville and that stupid security guard jumped over the wall and nearly shot his own reflection in the ornamental garden mirror? Remember that guy who invented a car flame-thrower to stop hijackers? Did you hear about the guys who held up a whole restaurant? And the ones who robbed an entire New Year's Eve party?

The soup was delicious, the main course apparently sublime. I don't remember a thing except fleeting tastes and grand gestures. The birthday girl, Nantie produced a bottle of fifteen-year-old Scotch and stiff ones were poured. The jokes got worse, the conversation more twisted, the weaker ones started leaving. At around 2am our last guest staggered into the night. Thanks for a lovely dinner, um well, you know what I mean, he muttered.

Max, B and I sat on the lounge floor slugging down sleeping pills with the last of the Scotch. 'You won't believe what I'm wearing underneath this,' said B, and he unbuttoned his denim shirt to reveal a T-shirt with a black and white graphic of a Glock. Welcome to South Africa, it said, duck motherfucker.

I think it was Charlie Chaplin who said that life is a tragedy close up but a comedy in long shot, which is eventually how I will come to feel about everything, but that Wednesday night I was rattled right down to my core. I never told anyone about my lifeline, but I kept thinking about it, picturing my hand smeared with spices over and over again, before the sleeping pills and Scotch started to take hold. 'I feel like I've been rhino-darted,' I said to B before I staggered into bed and fell into a deep and dreamless black sleep.

Chapter two

I like to think it was the sound of a forest fever tree leaf crashing on to the lawn that woke my grandmother Elsie Margaret Dickson, usually known as Ess, that glorious morning in 1932. I like to imagine she slipped happily out of bed, pulled the curtain aside, and gazed greedily out at the sunlight playing on the lawns of Lovely Cottage. Perhaps, however, she butted her curls deeper into the pillow and sighed and groaned and wished the day had not arrived.

The forest fever tree is endemic to the little farming district of Agatha, outside Tzaneen, and is my favourite tree – a bold and frivolous creature whose grandiose green leaves drop suddenly to the ground like exclamation marks. Elsie, a Wits graduate and journalist, in as much as women were allowed to be in those days, had come from Johannesburg to visit her younger sister Petie, and Petie's husband Botha de Meillon.

Popsa, as they called him, was an impassioned entomologist who

My grandmother Ess, 1945, aged 35

was waging a ferocious war against malaria and mosquitoes in the Lowveld, and an even more ferocious one against his colleague Dr Siegfried Annecke, who eventually shot himself in a granadilla field. One of my other relatives claimed to have heard the shot.

Popsa was plucked from the *platteland* as a small boy after a teacher was impressed by his mind and, after finishing school, started studying medicine at the University of the Witwatersrand. When the students got to do autopsies, however, he was presented with the cold and purpled corpse of recently hanged murderess Daisy de Melker, who had been found guilty of murdering her son and accused of murdering two husbands. He fainted at the sight and immediately took up entomology.

'As we explore the horizons of animal behaviour related to our own,' Popsa would quote with scientific fervour, 'we may all but ignore insect society. Their path took leave of ours too long ago, and has pursued its singular course through aeons beyond our infant comprehension ...'[1]

Popsa was entertaining, opinionated and extremely bright. Those were his only redeeming features as far as Ess was concerned. For the rest, he represented everything uncouth in their rarefied and socially complex Edwardian world. He was Afrikaans, he came from the Orange Free State, was strong jawed, ruddy cheeked and stubborn headed. He had the worst table manners she'd ever seen and he broke wind loudly without so much as an apology.

She was completely fascinated.

Ess and her elder sister Lala shared a house in Waterfall Avenue in Craighall Park in Johannesburg. Along with Petie, they too were finely featured, pale and pink-skinned, like lovely desserts, thought Popsa, with traces of strawberry in their hair and fine ginger freckles in interesting places. Lala was studying to be a

---

[1] Robert Ardrey, *The Hunting Hypothesis*.

concert pianist under the guidance of the dashing Rene Caprera of the Symphony Orchestra. Her instruction was causing great concern to the conductor's wife, it being obvious that Rene found her to be, well, good, really very good indeed. It was hard to resist a young Dickson, as Elsie Margaret was soon to discover, but in the meantime she put up with Lala's colourful descriptions of her piano lessons, and wondered nastily if Popsa had not married the more dull-minded of the sisters.

She had arrived the day before on the Zeederberg Coach, travelling first class of course. All the cheap seats got you was eighteen inches of bare wooden plank, while she at least had a backrest. And while ordinary wagons covered the distance between Pietersburg and Agatha in three days, the Zeederberg Coaches reduced the distance to an overnight journey.

The coach ran Monday, Wednesday and Friday, departing from Pietersburg at 9am. It was just a tiny *dorp* then, with unpaved streets, a handful of Indian-owned shops and a few buildings. The road took them past Zion City Moria, a prosperous religious settlement in the foothills of the Magoebaskloof mountains, and up into the cool slopes of Haenertsburg, where they overnighted at a simple hotel set against the backdrop of the Iron Crown mountain.

The next morning they wound their way down the precipitous slopes of the Magoebaskloof, emerging from the cool greenery into the hot basin of Lowveld heat that traps the town of Tzaneen like a fly in amber. From here they pushed up the slopes again, in a north east direction, where the forests once again thickened and it got cooler. Ess arrived at the New Agatha Hotel in the late afternoon, when the sun was kissing the mountains a slow orange farewell. The Coach House Hotel stands on this spot today, its uninterrupted mountain views still capable of bringing grown men to their knees.

The original hotel was built in 1888 as a staging post for the Zeederberg Coach Company, and from here the coach went on to

Leydsdorp, a small mining town in the Lowveld, where all that remains today is a shabby hotel and a cemetery whose headstones proclaim the loss of those who died of 'the fever'. They were heady days indeed, peppered with perilous incident and pioneering folk: fortune-seekers, gold prospectors, remittance men, renegades, filibusters and, of course, missionaries. There was malaria and blackwater fever; swamps and wild animals.

Ess was in no danger at all of course. 'Come in, dear, come in,' said Mrs Strachan, owner of the New Agatha Hotel, ushering her into the cheery lobby and introducing her briskly to Louis Thompson, District Surgeon of Leydsdorp, Mr Ward, the Inspector of Lands from Haenertsburg and Mr Beatty, the magistrate of Pietersburg. The men nodded, lifted their hats and returned to their conversation.

'Now be reasonable, Mrs S,' Thompson the surgeon said, clasping his hands together slowly. The men, it seemed, had brought a bottle of their own whisky to the hotel, from which they had had a nightcap before retiring. That morning they were astonished to find they had been charged for the half bottle they'd drunk – and to add insult to injury, the old tart Strachan had taken possession of the remaining half. She was about to begin her defence when Petie and Popsa arrived to fetch Ess.

They jiggled gently down to Lovely Cottage in a horse and cart. The views were glorious. The late afternoon light played piano on the spines of the mountains in notes of lilac and lavender, dove grey, dark blue. In the distance the mountains dropped away into the rolling Lowveld, punctuated by koppies and hills. Ess gazed in delight at this vast expanse of unexplored bush as her sister slapped an imaginary mosquito off her pale pink ankle.

Some low-lying pockets of the region are still known as 'fever belts' and the history of the Transvaal Lowveld is fraught with epidemics of malaria, cerebral malaria and blackwater fever, so named because it turns the sufferer's urine liquorice black. In a typical year, the dry Lowveld heat breaks around October with the first summer rains, a call to action for colonies of fever-bearing mosquitoes. By April, as the rains recede, the earth suppurates with swampy water creating the ideal breeding conditions for the *Anopheles* mosquito. Which was where Popsa entered.

The house in which he and Petie lived was called Lovely Cottage, and lovely it was, with a charming woodsy feel. There were plump armchairs, generous couches and a happy Dachsund called Dandy, short for Dandelion. The lounge was large, the kitchen sturdy. The spare room looked out on to the lawn, while the main bedroom was as big as a meadow, with dappled light and creeper-laced windows. Popsa showed Ess his study filled with books, boxes, files, glass cases and metal cabinets, microscopes, mosquito tanks, glass slides, pipettes. Then he opened a bottle of fine red and the three sat down and ate and drank until late in the evening, moving from table to fireside as the next bottle was uncorked.

When Popsa filled Ess's glass he did so with uncharacteristic tenderness, which went completely unnoticed by Petie, poor Petie.

'Tell me about yourself, Ess,' he said. 'I'm sure you are more fascinating than a million insects.'

'Oh indeed,' laughed my grandmother. 'The insect world may be older than us in evolutionary terms, but we have minds, we have consciousness.'

'Aah and we have consciences,' replied Popsa, gazing lustfully at her.

The next morning, that golden morning in May, Ess, Petie and Popsa walked over to Kings Walden to meet the owner of the farm, Mr Billo Tooley, who leased Lovely Cottage to Popsa. Calling for Dandy, they set off down a gentle grassy slope, across a pretty dam wall, up a jacaranda-lined road towards a large farmhouse. There they were met by Mr Tooley and his staff, and shown in.

In 1904 when he settled in Agatha, it was a wild, wild place. He bought some 800 hectares of land and named it Kings Walden after the village in Hertfordshire from which he'd come and where his parents ran the royal estate. Over the years he built up a fine farm that produced oranges, pecans, granadillas, avocados, litchis and tomatoes.

But it was the view that caught my grandmother's heart. Deep green forests danced at the feet of wild blue crags and purple cliffs. Banks of creamy clouds soothed the tops of brooding mountains. As long as I can remember, I've never known anyone not to let out a gasp at the sight of the view from Kings Walden. And Elsie Dickson was no different. She stood at the edge of the land, and from her beautiful O-shaped mouth slipped a delicate gasp. A rash of goosebumps broke out on her slender forearm, like a breeze rippling the surface of a lake.

Billo Tooley was completely enchanted.

He called for the maids to bring out tea served on the Royal Doulton, he called for welcoming sherries in crystal glasses, he called for refreshments on silver plates, he called for them all to hurry and, as he strode towards the young Elsie hovering deliciously at the viewpoint, he called out a silent cry of thanks to the Lord above.

'To the right, my dear,' he began, 'are the highest reaches of the northern range, mysterious and folded, the source of many rivers, headwaters of the Letsitele. They are home to many a cave and secret pool. The uppermost peak is known by the locals as Serala, we call it Kruger's Head. Those are the Twelve Apostles, those are the Downs, that is Cypress Point ...'

But Elsie Dickson was listening with only half an ear. When she was ten years old, Elsie fell into a big loamy hole in her parents' garden in Johannesburg – she was stuck there for many hours – but instead of experiencing fear and claustrophobia, the event imparted to her the gift of what we gardeners call Planter's Hands. Everything she planted grew, and her fingers ached as she strolled around Kings Walden's grounds.

Cool breezes ruffled the topknots of the trees, the Lowveld shimmered below. It made her eyes water to look there, as if she'd had a double gin. In her mind she imagined fiery poinsettias, blazing red-hot pokers, orange-pink begonias, marmalade bushes. Billo pointed out his orchards and pack sheds, his latest plans and schemes. The shadow of a crested eagle fell across their path as they walked. Grasses tickled their ankles. A frog flopped lazily into a puddle.

'Oh, it's so beautiful here!' cried Elsie as they completed their walk. 'I never want to leave.'

To which my grandfather Billo replied: 'Marry me and you'll never have to.'

My grandfather Billo

Chapter three

It is this romantic spirit that draws me back to Kings Walden after the robbery even though, ironically, my own marriage collapses and everything I know about my life and self is cleaved into a Before The Armed Robbery and an After. I feel as if I have stepped off a long journey aboard a ship. The trauma causes within me an acute and intense need to live life immediately without any hesitation.

I strike towards the unclaimed like a cobra.

The first to go is my marriage, my dreadful marriage. A struggling, traumatised, uneven and essentially mismatched affair, I destroy it around me, like a firefighter killing a series of runaway bushfires. I cannot bear this perceived captivity any longer, I just want out, for ever, now, if not sooner.

'You'll never find a man who loves you as much as I do,' screams my husband.

We are in a borrowed car. I am returning him to his mother.

'I need out,' I scream back.

Then the car splutters and jerks and stops. It's a breakdown. B gets out and kicks the car door and shouts 'fuck, fuck, fuck!' I flick the car radio on.

The first time ever I saw your face, sings Shirley Bassey, *I felt the earth moooooooove …*

I call a friend. We stand angrily on the side of the road without facing each other until she arrives. I get into her car without saying a word to B. In the rear-view mirror I see him standing alone on the side of the road, like a country and western song, all alone with a broken heart and a broken-down car. I am remorseless.

I put the Joburg house on the market, arrange storage for my furniture, and head like a homing pigeon back to the land of my ancestors. In my ocean of desperation the farm and the mountains offer not only an exit plan but they symbolise the only constant in my tumultuous life.

All I want to do is sit on the stoep of the old Kings Walden farmhouse and stare at the mountains, my mountains, the ones at which I have stared throughout my life. The Northern Drakensberg mountains have been there for millions of years, 'a glorious geological fault dividing the Highveld plateau from the coastal plains of the Lowveld; a colossal marble cake created by a series of primordial upheavals'.[2]

It is towards these mountains that I barrel at dawn, in a borrowed car, a refugee from my own life. I'm clinging to the steering wheel with one hand and, with the other, the ends of a cappuccino and yet another cigarette. My mind is pumping with a brain load of

---

[2] Peter Joyce, *Golden Escarpment*.

scrambled and violent staccato images and it takes about ten minutes before I have to pull over and burst into tears. It's not just post-traumatic stress though, but early conditioning too.

My first travel memories are of leaving our home in Craighall Park, Johannesburg, in the back of the Peugeot station wagon with my older brother Brett upfront, and Steven, the middle child, and me, the youngest, in the back. Steven always ate all the *padkos* before we reached the top of Bompas Road and I always cried before we reached William Nicol Drive. There were bitter feuds, salty tears, recriminations and threats by our parents that we would have to get out and walk.

I'm shaking like a leaf when I manage to slide back on to the M1 and still jittery and jumpy as I take the hairpin bend turn-off on to the N1 to Polokwane. I scratch for the required R5.40 – what a silly amount – at the first toll plaza, the coins are trapped somewhere in the dregs of my still wallet-less, cellphone-less handbag, furry with sweat and bits of tobacco. But it's like breaking through a psychological barrier as the red-striped pole lifts up and I drive out into the open space north east of Pretoria, an area once called the Springbok Flats.

There are early accounts by farmers of this part of the Waterberg area that tell of the massive herds of springbok that migrated across the veld. One farmer described how it took more than a week for one herd to rumble past his farmstead. Now there are taxis clattering past at breakneck speed, packed with resigned and anxious looking passengers, dick-swingers in flashy new cars that bear down like maniacs from a Mad Max movie, sales reps zipping past eating takeaways and talking on their mobiles ... I'm unable to cope with the fast lane, and stick to the left, gazing out the window on to this surreal road movie. Above the soft mountains in the distance I see vultures wheeling in the skies and decide to turn off on to the R101 to Bela-Bela.

This is the Old Road, the one we used to take to Go Up North – even though it was in fact Down, as my father would point out.

Back then the trip was a mammoth six and a half hour undertaking which generally left everyone in a state of emotional devastation. I can recall a few warm fluffy moments, I think, of feeling safe and snug under the blanket in the back of the car as roadside stalls, game fences and road signs slipped past. But my sense of safety existed only as long as we were moving. The signs outside pointed to towns where the old flag flew high, alongside the soaring steeples of Calvinist churches. We were told terrible stories as children – mainly by my parents and the turfy clutch of English-speaking residents of Agatha – about the inbred and backward Afrikaners who apparently lurked in these little towns, stories about *boeremusiek, sjamboks* and brandied moustaches breathing heavily on prepubescent girls and cowering blacks.

The only thing I liked about these towns was the defiant bloom of *kaffirbome*, as they were called, although this was definitely not considered Polite in our household, nor Scientific for that matter. The coral tree is classified *Erythrina lysistemon*, my father would say firmly, 'and that is that'.

The Old Road took us from Warmbaths, Nylstroom, Naboomspruit, Potgietersrus and Pietersburg to Tzaneen. Today the same road heads through Bela-Bela, Modimolle, Mookgopong, Mokopane and Polokwane, an onomatopoeic incantation of reclamation, a rhythm of African change that has long been beaten upon this landscape, long before *oranje, blanje, blou* and all those bastards. I'm not sure how to reconcile that hideous past with my discombobulated and surreal present. The car radio is playing Phala Phala FM and I'm suddenly rigid with fear at the thought that the guys who put a gun to my head are out there somewhere listening to the same music, sliding around in some oily, stinky crack-shack in Alex. This very Saturday morning.

It has been a week or two since the robbery. I'm still wobbly and my peripheral vision is heightened, animal sharp. I'm keenly aware of every motion around me, and anything sudden brings wild shock. It's a buzzing Saturday morning in Bela-Bela where I stop to buy cheap sunglasses and water. The whole town is going through the usual jigga-jigga of shopping, eating, chatting, jaywalking and driving around in the wrong lane. At the bottom end of town the main road is lined with chain stores and Amper Mahala (next to nothing) shops, bakeries, butcheries, muti shops and cellphone outlets. The pavements are crowded with hawkers selling everything from cheap T-shirts imported from Asia to braids, beads and pink plastic mirrors.

'Hola, baba,' I say to the attendant when I stop for petrol.

'Go bjang?' he says. (How are you?) He has short dreadlocks, a laid-back face. *'O ya kae?'* (Where are you going?)

'Gae ke kae?' he asks. (Where's home?)

'Agatha, ka ntle ga Tzaneen,' I say wearily. (Agatha, just outside Tzaneen.)

'Eish, ke tswa Nkowankowa,' he says, laughing, *'kua fase.'* (I'm from Nkowankowa just down the road.) *'Ke kabaka la eng le tloga toropong ye kgolo mma?'* (Why are you running from the big city, mammie?)

In the middle of town I drive past the Royal Hotel. Sometimes when we were little, en route to Tzaneen, we would be taken to tea here, after we had swum at the nearby Hot Springs. The springs are now centrepiece for a busy Aventura Resort. Back then, they were a jealously guarded hideout of local Afrikaners who tolerated our visits with as much disdain as we tolerated their presence. My grandmother would seat herself imperiously on a bench and watch us swim. My mother was once asked to leave because she was wearing a bikini. Brett was three at the time and naked.

'Skies mevrou.' A crimplene-clad tannie with breadstick legs came

shuffling up to my mother, who had carefully and evenly applied fake tan and was spread out on her back in the sun.

'*Skies mevrou, maar die bestuurder sê bikinis is nie toegelaat nie.*' (Excuse me, but the manager says no bikinis are allowed.) She was holding a big book covered in fabric, which no doubt was filled with rules and regulations because she tapped it officiously and repeated in slightly shriller tones:

'*Mevrou ... die bikinis is heeltemaal nie toegelaat nie. Asseblief. En die bestuurder sê dat die kind ook klere moet dra.*'

She gazed venomously at the naked Brett, who squinted in the sunlight, toying with his tiny penis.

My mother stood up slowly. Panther-like, she drew herself up to her full height – she's nearly six foot – carefully adjusted her tiny bikini, tossed back her mane of long dark hair and, with a disdainful and haughty look, slowly walked once around the breadstick lady, who stood in her floral crimplene dress feeling short and fat and trounced.

From Bela-Bela, the road leads past grape farms, citrus estates, *vakansie oorde* and *wildtuine* towards Modimolle. I'm amazed to see some of them are still there, like the *Hotspot Padstal* which is now draped in a flamboyant show of orange honeysuckle and painted with zebra stripes. I pass the selfsame old fig tree under which we used to stop for tea from a Thermos Flask, which was poured into Proper Cups and served with condensed milk.

The new name at the entrance to the town has simply been mounted over the old one and stands rather drearily atop its monstrous face brick plinth. I stop at a bottle store on the outskirts of town and buy two cold quarts of *Zamalek* and press on, bleary-eyed, towards the old Naboomspruit, now named Mookgopong, thinking cynically that this particular name swap was a real lose-lose situation for everyone, especially western tourists.

There are plastic bags fluttering like trapped birds in the roadside thorn trees. I pass the Monate New Testament Church, the Jaagbaan Guesthouse, a sign to Country Music Farm, and a *bosveld* B&B which has a big cross on its roof and an ox wagon wheel on the lawn. I feel like I'm caught somewhere in the seventies, time of the ultimate mixed message.

On the one hand the country was in the tightening grip of Afrikaner Nationalism, boys my age were prancing round in khaki, practising for Veld School or the army and we were enduring an education that preached the stork and the ox wagon. And on the other hand, my parents were busy discovering their personal freedom following the fallout of the sixties' cultural revolution which reached South Africa in a limited way and in their lives boiled down to three essential things – the invention of birth control, the advent of the bikini, and the consumption of the gallon bottle of wine.

It was common knowledge in the neighbourhood that the Hilton-Barber parents were amongst the wildest. They were young, liberal, bohemian. My father David worked in PR, public relations, and had big curly hair and the latest seventies' jackets in velvet and suede. My mother Tana wore as little as possible.

She had a silver chain welded around her waist by a little old Jewish jeweller in Rosebank, where she took Steven and me one afternoon after we'd been to the Rosebank Library and to Clarks for new school shoes. Oh how his hands trembled as he soldered that slender chain round that slender waist. One Christmas we were renovating, a frequent feature of our young lives, and Tana walked naked across the scaffolding in the lounge to the sounds of Jesus Christ Superstar, which was banned. *Prove to me that you're no fool*, she sang loudly, *Walk across my swimming pool . . .*

We lived in a big thatched home in Craighall Park, Johannesburg, There were three children. Brett, the eldest, five years older than me, the most cunning but least wild; Steven, the middle one, eighteen

The three Hilton-Barber children, Craighall house, 1967

months my senior, most charming and wildest, blackest of the black sheep; and me, the only-blonde-only-girl-child, hardy perennial and unsurprisingly the most skilled in observation and manipulation. I worshipped the ground upon which my brothers walked.

Brett, Steven and I seldom got fed on weekends, but during the week we underwent a culinary exploration unheard of in the suburbs. While everyone else was having takeaways, a new phenomenon, the Hilton-Barber children's palates were being tested on a range of dishes from Italy, France, the Middle East, North Africa, the Caribbean, China and beyond. My mother went to endless cooking lessons, returning flushed, jolly and inspired. We had clam bakes, fondue evenings, cassoulets, pâtés, roulades, chickens baked in mud casing and once even a real glazed pig with an apple stuffed in its mouth. Tana was only once forced to temporarily rein in her exotic-ness. That was following the presentation of a Tuscan-style baked rabbit on the dining room table which caused Steven to burst into loud sobs. 'Flopsy and Mopsy,' he choked, 'Cottontail ...'

My parents tried to brew their own lager in the room downstairs – it was called Pepperillo's Room, after one of our dogs – and my father even designed a label for the brew, which was going to be called Barber Lager, but the still blew up and so they returned with gusto to wine by the gallon and took up the guitar. They had a bearded teacher called Jannie Bezuidenhout, an avuncular chap who endured their musical efforts with humour and grace. They played songs from Nina and Frederick, Dionne Warwick, The Beatles, Bob Dylan, the Mamas and the Papas. My father sang beautifully, my mother with more passion than tune. Her voice rose as the level of the wine bottle dropped, and sometimes she would let her long hair down and howl like a jackal ... *'It's a lesson too late for the learning, made of sand, made of sand ...'*

Our garden was huge with peach trees and plum trees and an underground cellar and a fort that my mother built at the bottom of the garden. We had alarmingly few boundaries in our lives and the only time I got a real hiding was when I destroyed my mother's elephant ear patch so that Steven and I could play elephants. For the rest of the time we were free to frolic, shoot birds with pellet guns, shoot each other, make revolting concoctions to throw on to the neighbour's veranda, experiment with chlorine smoke bombs, burn our Barbie dolls and terrorise each other. I was the frequent victim of knives, sticks, cricket balls, soil clods, and lassos. I was stabbed in the leg, shot in the foot with a pellet gun and knocked clean out when a flying cricket ball hit me on the back of the head from close range.

'Oh bloody hell, would you look at that!' shrieked my mother one Saturday afternoon. 'Dave, Dave, look at the children.' Brett was having a birthday party in the garden; he must have been nine or ten, and my parents and I had gone for a walk to the café to get them cigarettes. Now we were in the kitchen overlooking the garden.

A small dark-haired boy was vomiting next to the pool. Two little girls were pulling each other's hair. A gang of rosy-cheeked boys fought and rolled and giggled on the grass, another little girl was crying, Brett was hitting a friend with a bamboo stick. A gallon bottle of wine lay empty on the grass ...

'They've drunk all the wine,' gasped my father, 'and their parents are coming to fetch them any minute ...'

The effects of our family's wild reputation were keenly felt in the suburb. My brothers' special, saddle-less bicycle with no brakes – The Castration Machine – was known with fear by every little boy from Craighall Park to Blairgowrie. One of my school friends tried to ride it and broke both her arms after she slammed into a brick wall. She was banned from ever seeing me again. We were shunned by most PTAs, school committees, cubs, brownies and every other parents' association within a fifty kilometre radius. Brett was removed from confirmation classes when the priest told him animals have no souls. 'What about Mazabuka?' said my mother, clutching her Burmese cat to her bosom. 'You are never to go near that evil man again.'

Unsurprisingly, I never took to school and my mother disregarded school holidays, taking us up to Kings Walden as often as she could. The farm was a refuge from 12 Northumberland Avenue and its attendant politics. As I travel along the old road, it follows the names of the stations we used to pass on childhood journeys with The Railways, as my grandmother called the South African Railway Service. We travelled first class, of course, even though it was actually a milk train and would take twenty-four hours to get to Tzaneen from Joburg. But it was Civilised and Clean which was very important, and we were waved out of Park Station in Johannesburg from the Whites Only end of the platform and chugged our way out through townships and shacks and peri-urban villages, slowly towards the bushveld with its flat-topped acacias and blonde grasslands that promised delicious possibility.

The milk train really did stop at all the stops. Squeaking and hissing and puffing it delivered milk to Warmbaths, Hammanskraal, Moordrift, Eerstelingsrivier, Tobias, Sandrivier, Nylstroom, Rooipoort, Potgietersrus, Pietersburg, Munnik, Moeketsi, Politsi. Tana would open a bottle of wine as soon as the train started moving and Steven and I would be left to wreak havoc on the monkey ropes, skateboard up and down the passages, or run up and down and play *tok-tokkie* on closed compartment doors. Brett would drive up with my father and meet us at the other end.

The small town stations where we stopped were redolent with red stoep polish and racism. The black passengers – Non-Europeans as they were known then, swept to the back of the train and the fringes of society with a simple prefix – had separate gates and were crammed on to hard wooden benches in third class, along with their children, sacks of mielie meal, blankets, boxes, pumpkins and of course chickens. Chickens have always been acceptable passengers on South African trains, even in first class. We sometimes brought chickens back from the farm, and kept them in our garden in Craighall Park. There was one called Matilda the Hen that regularly laid eggs in my father's armchair in the lounge.

The stationmaster would bark out commands to Boys – everyone called them boys, these men – who were dressed in colonial khaki and pronked about like the springboks that were the emblem of The Railways and frosted on to its train windows. Shaded by the proverbial flame or flamboyant tree, the station buildings were government green-and-beige, with wooden swing doors that opened into a room with flourishing pot plants, polished wooden counters and pictures of Prime Minister John Vorster.

It was during my travels on The Railways that I learnt about the gay underground subculture that apparently flourished to the clickety clack of wheels on the track. My mother has always adored gay men – 'They would never wear crimplene,' she said, as if that explained everything. She adored glam, camp or any combination thereof, and loved the drama and fuss that would be made as we stopped at the stations. She swung elegantly from train to platform, watched by the other passengers with a mixture of admonishment and admiration, into the embrace of some impeccably uniformed and heavily moustached man called Gerrie or Bokkie or Almer or, mysteriously, Millie.

'*Ooooh hullooooo Mevrou Yilton-Baaaaba,*' the steward would shriek as he saw her approach. There would be a lot of wrist flapping and air kissing and he would call for refreshments and backup.

'*Kom, kom, laat ons 'n bietjie warm tee of koffie drink? Of miskien vir mejuvrou a glassie wyn nè?*' said with a wink.

They knew her preferences, and she theirs. Steven and I called them *koffiemoffies* and he said that when they weren't on the train they dressed up like the Village People and performed unspeakable acts with young black boys and other men. I was intrigued and confused. These were the same stewards that offered us impeccable service as we travelled, service of which even my grandmother approved. They could serve peas while going through a tunnel without spilling a single one.

My mother Tana, 1968, Johannesburg

In the evenings, one of them came along and produced, from a long blue, sausage-shaped canvas bag, a ready-made bed with sheets and blankets that unfolded out on to the bunk. He pulled up the metal windows, pulled down the canvas blinds and showed us how to put on the night light. Then the refreshments man came swaying down the corridor, rattling his key in the compartment doors and shouting out: 'Tea, coffee, something from the bar', and Tana would get more wine and we would get very sweet tea with Cremora sachets that were 'new on the market' and considered very sophisticated.

Later in the inky night we lay snug in our SARS papooses listening to the sounds outside amplify and recede. The clatter of milk cans, Afrikaans commands, Sotho muttering, sounds that rose and fell as we chuffed and shunted and hissed. I tried not to think of the heinous homosexual acts of which Steven spoke, or the *tsotsis*, about whom I had recently read in Alan Paton's *Cry, the Beloved Country*.

I'm still trying not to think about them today.

From Mokopane and Polokwane, the road takes me, as it took my grandmother, past the settlements around Zion City Moria and up into the hills of the Magoebaskloof mountains. I wonder if she had any idea whatsoever about the outcome of her first visit to Agatha? I have powerful recollections of her, dressed in a linen suit to match her powder-blue Ford Ranchero, fetching us at one or other little station siding, with her Boys to help load up. She was a terrible driver, fond of overtaking on blind rises, forcing other cars off the road with death-defying acts of speed and performing random forays on to the verges, especially in the mist.

My grandmother always enjoyed a good time, preferably at someone else's expense and especially so in the later years of her life when she went quite mad. She lived all alone on the farm for nearly forty years after her husband Billo died. She would walk daily with her stick and little dog Darling and at night she would stand on the stoep with a sherry and beaten egg (her staple at that stage) and point to the flickering lights of Nkowankowa township and then to the dark hills of nothingness. 'Those are the lights,' she would say, 'and that is the void.'

She would frequently receive imaginary guests who had flown in on the Venda Tray, an extraordinary aircraft that did New York to Venda – an admittedly unusual route – in a matter of hours. When the nearby Coach House Hotel was being built, she marched down to the site and fired the entire workforce. She took instant dislikes to people. Many of my friends and brothers' girlfriends were accused of being trollops and strumpets and chased out of the house. She once prevented a boyfriend from leaving on 'her' motorbike. The ageing gardener, who had walked all the way from Malawi to South Africa as a seventeen-year-old, had doors slammed in his face and resorted to mowing the lawn at night with a torch strapped on to his head. 'Oh look, here comes that dreadful drunk,' my granny would say as my father returned, rosy-cheeked, from a walk.

I drive through the town of Tzaneen and then finally up the road to Agatha, past the Flora Café, past the station and the industrial area, past the black whores at the bottom of the road dressed in tiny pink hot pants and strappy orange sundresses with Jackie O glasses and cheerful umbrellas. I drive up into the hills, past familiar homesteads shaded by ancient exotic trees; past the signs for pack houses, banana loading points and compounds.

By the time I get to the turn-off to Kings Walden I am exhausted. I have finally, tearfully and wearily reached my sanctuary. Nostalgia, beer and the thought of seeing my dear parents alive, and being able to put my arms around them finally, physically, actually, renders me helpless. I stop and get out at the top of the avenue, hot and sobbing, and have a cigarette and look out across the hills and mountains. 'I gaze upon the distant hills from whence my help cometh,' I say aloud, dramatically quoting Job of all things, and then get into the car and drive down to my ancestral home.

Chapter four

An elegant assortment of cars began trundling down the driveway to Kings Walden in 1933 as my grandmother Ess Tooley slid herself into her wedding dress and gazed into the mirror on her dressing table. It was a large framed mirror with two side mirrors, so that if she adjusted it just right, she was reflected infinitely, like an endless chorus line of lovely brides. The new Mrs Tooley had beautiful cheekbones and an unruly look in her eye.

'Why wait?' she said cheerily to just about everyone she could about the speed with which she was upping, marrying and leaving Johannesburg. Billo was handsome and charming and wealthy and he adored her. Yes, he was twenty years older, but then why should that get in the way of a grand life and a beautiful home in one of the *most* glorious places you've ever seen? Oh how her fingers ached as she thought of that fertile soil, that enchanting aspect of land. And, what's more, her sister and her husband were right next door!

Billo and Ess were married on the lawns of Kings Walden,

overlooking the mountains that change every day. Her sisters were bridesmaids. Petie, the middle sister, was a petite and pretty redhead. Lala, the oldest sister, was a taller and better looking brunette, and most dramatic of the three sisters. She was smoking a cigarette with a long black holder, and was going to play the piano for the wedding guests later on.

'I should have married Henry,' said Lala, in her low voice.

Lala was a concert pianist and one of the first woman broadcasters at Slezingers, forerunner of the SABC, and she played the piano and talked and sang under the name of Aunty Lex. Part of her act was a little dog called Henry, a fat white terrier with bright black eyes, who was a mascot at the Cape Town studios when he was a puppy. That was until Lala laid eyes on him, scooped him up and accompanied him as he became the first South African dog to be televised, ride in a speedboat, play the piano and fly in a Puss Moth. Henry met Governors General and Cabinet Ministers, shook hands – er, paws – with King Edward VIII, Conan Doyle and Bernard Shaw.

'His father's name was Arrigo Alcohol,' Lala said. 'What breeding! Imagine, if I'd married him I would have been called Lala Alcohol – what a stage name!'

She flung her arms in the air and the ash from her cigarette fell to the floor.

Lala had several photo albums devoted to Henry and far more photographs of him than of her husband Tom, and anyway she was still having an affair with Caprera of the Symphony Orchestra. Henry, Lala and Caprera travelled some fifty thousand miles in his motor car and had all recently flown over Cape Town in a Puss Moth.

'The sensation of speed is soooooo exhilarating,' said Lala. 'Henry jumped in as if he had been accustomed to flying his whole life and he wasn't even put off by the association with cats.'

Popsa and Petie in Burma in the 1930s

'It's far more comfortable than a motor car,' she continued enthusiastically as her sister gazed into her infinite mirror, 'and one of the great advantages of course is that one can smoke in the cabin. There is no fear of fire on a long journey since the petrol tank is in the wings.' She drained her glass of champagne. 'And it only takes eight hours and thirty-five minutes for a Puss Moth to fly from Johannesburg to Cape Town!'

'Enough about you and Henry,' said Petie. 'I can't believe you're going on about a terrier and a Puss Moth when our sister is getting married.'

'What else shall we talk about?' retorted Lala. 'How about sex?'

All three sisters giggled.

'Oh Essie, please don't be one of those wives who lies back and thinks of England,' said Lala waving her empty glass at her beribboned sister. 'Take it slowly, take it easily, you are the leading actress in a *film noir* in which the heroine gets seduced by a handsome beast ...'

But the new Mrs Tooley thought of gardening and took to sex like the proverbial duck to water. Her new life at Kings Walden was excellent. The farmhouse was very well positioned, spacious and gracious. In true colonial style, the kitchen was as far away as possible from the dining room, so that the ringing of a small silver bell was followed by the satisfying scurry of servants' feet.

Ess and Billo had separate bedrooms. Hers had glass doors that opened out on to the lawn, swimming pool and the tennis court and clubhouse beyond. Her bedroom was flooded with sunshine in the mornings and the forest fever trees threw interesting shadows in the yellow-green afternoons. Billo's bedroom looked on to the mountains of course, a view that unfailingly brought a faraway look into my grandmother's eyes, which my grandfather conveniently mistook for true love.

My great-aunt Lala and Henry

They exchanged visits to each other's bedrooms with great delight, and met on the stoep overlooking the mountains every evening for a drink as night fell and the breeze carried faint scents of woodsmoke and cut grass. A sherry for her and a Scotch for him. 'Up to the pretty,' he said to himself, as he poured whisky and water three quarters of the way up the crystal glass, where the pattern began.

'Your garden is going to look lovely, Elsie darling,' said Billo tenderly, commenting on the new stone wall that had been built at the edge of the view. It certainly hadn't taken her long to don her hat, gloves and attitude and set about instructing the builders and gardeners.

She ordered the mass planting of poinsettias, bougainvillea and red-hot pokers for the winter months, and carefully positioned shady trees for the hot subtropical summers. She planted pink Brazilian kapoks, purple jacarandas from South America, red flame trees from Australia, pink tibouchinas from South America. The soil was excellent in Agatha and everything grew very well. Her kitchen garden was flourishing, and to keep away the monkeys and guard the vegetables, she'd engaged the help of a pretty young thing called Melea Letsoalo, daughter of one of the farm workers.

'I have such grand plans,' sighed Ess. 'Don't you just love your fountain?'

'I am honoured and flattered,' replied Billo. His new wife had made him a fountain with a stone spitting lion that trickled into a low pond, surrounded with ferns and embellished with honeysuckle. She took a photograph of him standing proudly in front of his Hudson Terraplane in front of the fountain, the only sign of his driver Hatry a telltale white glove resting on the back of the car.

Billo had appointed Hatry to be the driver of the Hudson and dressed him in a fine white suit. Hatry's job included serving my grandfather drinks and refreshments en route, and for this purpose, the Hudson was equipped with a pull-out drinks cabinet in the back seat. Before stepping into the car with Hatry, however, Billo would first conduct the Armpit Test, an extremely undignified exercise that consisted of him sniffing Hatry's armpit to check for offensive body odour.

'I don't want to travel with the attar of Africa in the Hudson,' he said, 'even if it is just to the local store, never mind all the way through the Springbok Flats to Johannesburg.'

Hatry took a photograph of my grandparents together in front of the Hudson. Billo wore khaki and tweed and the self-satisfied air of a country squire whose dogs are trained, crops sprayed and natives disciplined. Ess wore a flared pants suit and Jackie O sunglasses. They are holding hands and smiling.

Billo was both startled and delighted to discover that his new wife was passionate, intelligent and independent. She insisted on learning to drive, which was a terrifying affair as the Hudson galloped down the avenue, Billo clutching his gin, Hatry tight-lipped and disapproving in the back.

Billo watched the mountains change from purple to charcoal, saw the faintest glimmer of lights in the distant foothills. He listened to the rising chorus of frogs and the chirrup of crickets. He heard the sound of a lone hadeda heading home much later than the others, and gazed at his young wife in the fading pink light talking about her plans for planting hibiscus and goodness knows what else.

'Elsie, my darling,' he said, gently taking her hand. 'Would you like to dance?'

And as the servants dashed quietly about preparing final touches for dinner, Billo put on the gramophone and they danced on the stoep as the sweet scent of jasmine and desire filled the Agatha evening.

My mother Tana was born the following April, a fiercely pretty

Hatry the driver

dark-haired girl with intense eyes and eyebrows.

'She is going to be a tough one, *wendziba wena*,' said Mama Gidjane, one of the garden workers, to Melea, whom Ess now appointed to look after her newly born daughter. *'Jo, jo, jo, jo,'* replied Melea. 'You think her life will not be good?' 'This one carries the sad spirit of the ancestors,' said Mama Gidjane. 'Her life will not be easy.' She shook her head and took the baby girl from Melea and held her protectively to her breast.

Billo was sixty-something when Tana was born, and he instructed the building of a *rondavel* overlooking the mountains so the mewling young thing did not disturb him. It was a simple thatch room, but the view was soothing and it provided a social nexus for the young Melea and Mama Gidjane who ferried the baby around on their backs, or laid blankets on the long green lawn across which she was made to crawl, determined legs, dark eyebrows.

Shortly after Tana was born, Petie and Popsa, who were still living next door at Lovely Cottage, produced two little girls, Mimi and Delia, enchanting things, all smiley and wriggly and showing signs of sunny dispositions that later turned into great artistic talent. The three girls spent a great deal of time together in the Kings Walden garden, which my grandmother lovingly recorded in a series of photograph albums showing the three little girls at tea parties, on the lawn, under the trees, generally naked except for their bonnets.

It meant less washing, she said to Billo who wondered about naked girl children and etiquette. His new wife plainly preferred gardening to motherhood and domesticity. Every morning she would get dressed – big hat, sunglasses, elegantly tapered trousers – and get out into the garden where she would boss around the garden workers in a manner that left no doubt as to who was in charge.

'Move that, you silly man. No, not like that! Come along now, I said put that tree over there ...'

Fortunately there was a bevy of staff to handle domesticity. There was always washing, lots of it, and no electricity, no lights, no irons, fridges or stoves. The water was pumped straight out of the river. Every evening the paraffin lamps were lit, water for the bath was heated by a fire in the outside donkey and the house was sprayed against malaria. The little girls played piano for their parents, drinks would tinkle, dinner would be served and Melea and the other servants would slip like ghosts into the African night.

Chapter five

My African ghosts are a different beast. I am wracked with trauma and despair within the first few days of arriving back at Kings Walden. I camp unhappily in one of the outside guest rooms – it's called Modjadji because of the ancient cycad that guards the door – and generally clutching the beginning or end of a bottle of wine, until my father bravely decides to take action and drives to Joburg to collect the cats who are still in the Joburg house, alone but being fed by a friend.

Even braver, however, is my mother, who will have them as guests. No one dare contest the supremacy of her enormous Siamese whose name is Dr Zambuk. The good doctor is most concerned at the arrival of his quivering city cousins and takes to yowling loudly and flinging himself against the closed door of the Modjadji suite like a creature possessed. 'Perhaps he needs to administer an operation,' my mother says jokingly, but we are all taking strain.

Brett says when he dies he wants to come back as a cat at Kings

Walden. Tana's cats are immensely spoiled. They are brushed three hundred times each night and lie around in the day like demigods. Joyce, chief matron of the guesthouse kitchen, brings bowls of steamed hake or chicken which they are fed on the dining room table, in the bedroom, on the dressing table, even on the bed. My father's protests have long been ignored. Once I brought a boyfriend home and he watched in horror as the cats' fish came out of the fridge. 'At our house,' he said in disbelief, 'that kind of fish was a family treat on Friday nights.'

And then, cleverly, my parents decide to go away for a few days and I am left with the feuding felines and the guesthouse, which is a good way, my father suggests, 'of taking your mind off things'. 'Don't mention the robbery,' says Tana cheerily as they leave. 'Are you sure you will be all right?'

I make my first mistake by going out for lunch and drinking wine. By the time I return I am filled with delight at the prospect of visitors. Half an hour later I am dying for a nap but dare not lie down since they may arrive any minute. I make my second mistake by having another glass of wine. I am extremely friendly – perhaps even overbearing – when they finally arrive a few hours and another few glasses later. But they turn out to be a convivial bunch from Botswana and their travel tiredness is instantly forgotten once they lay their eyes on the view and their hands on a drink.

The only hiccup happens when I am in the kitchen and see, out of the corner of my eye, the security guard Elias Mhlongo slink past with his shotgun. I shriek like a banshee, and the dogs and Joyce come running. 'It's ... it's nothing,' I say, biting back the tears and embarrassment. 'I just got a fright.' Everyone nods solemnly. Fortunately the guests are bathing and out of earshot. 'I'm sorry I shouted,' I say to Elias after I regroup, and tell him as simply as I can that I had been robbed at gunpoint and that it would probably be best if he called out my name as he approached.

I have known Elias the security guard for years. He lived in a room outside Hunters Moon, Brett's house further up the hill, when I lived there a few years ago. I would watch him from the stoep, outside his hut, wearing his Tarzan vest and holding a little enamel mug. He charged his cellphone in my kitchen and took random shots at the monkeys with his shotgun. Once he came down with a mysterious knee ailment. 'She's hot, she's burning,' he said, wincing and making pained expressions. He had slipped, it seemed, somewhere near the gate in the dark night, in the line of duty, and done something awful to his knee. I dropped him at the local hospital and he reappeared later with a sheepish look and a brown bag of medicine.

It turned out be to gout. The doctor told him to no longer 'eat the meat of the cow or drink the beer'. 'Feesh, she's OK,' said Elias, 'and the chiggen and the meat of the peengy.' I bought him a knee guard from Lombard's Chemist which he stared at for a long time, slowly saying the word 'support' over and over again with the same incredulous look on his face I get when I see a brand new Prado.

The next night there is no one at the guesthouse, so I send the staff off early and am left alone in the ancestral homestead, all alone for the first time in years and years. I head instinctively towards the dining room, which used to be my and Steven's bedroom. Brett was older and usually stayed in the outside cottage with his friends. Where guests now enjoy four-course gourmet meals, we once had our two little single beds with green bedspreads trimmed with white bobbles. Where the bar is now used to be the old boiler room with a donkey that used to fire up the water. 'Now that's a sign of progress,' Steven said when our old bedroom was first converted into a bar and dining room.

Framed black and white photographs of my ancestors line the cool white walls of the dining room which, like all good dining rooms, has no electric lighting and is lit only by lamps, candles and the odd serviette set aflame during a lively dinner. Bad light kills conversation, Tana always says. And doesn't everyone look better by candlelight?

The ancestors certainly do. This arrangement of fifty or so photo-graphs occupies an entire length of wall alongside the dining room table. They spill over on to the antique dresser, climb above the door frame and around the corner towards the bar as if in search of drink and cheer. There are photographs of my parents, brothers, grandfathers and their mothers, assorted aunts, uncles, second cousins, good friends, pets, maids, farm workers – a collection of ancestral butterflies, pinned to the wall for our dining pleasure.

In the centre is a photograph of my grandfather Billo, full name William Edwin Tooley. He has a broad gentle face, a side parting in his hair and he beams benevolently down on to the candles and flowers that eternally grace the table, although we all know he is turning furiously in his grave at how his beloved Kings Walden has been whittled down to a garden and a guesthouse. Not even the family cemetery belongs to the family any more! But the wine still flows like the Letaba River and, as they say around here, once you have tasted its waters, you will never leave. At least, you won't be able to stand up straight after dinner with the family in the ancestral dining room.

The ancestors love it when laughter fills the room. When the cutlery crashes, glasses drop to the ground and conversations rise and fall like empires, they look out happily from behind their frames, even the stiff Victorian oldies. Like Great Granny on my mother's side, who visibly exhales under her starched white bodice at the first sound of music. And Great Granny on my father's side – she grew to be one hundred and four years old – who smiles from behind her wrinkles like a happy Pekinese.

The velvet-skinned Lala looks down from her silver frame, all jazz era elegance and enigma. She needed little encouragement to party. Like my brother Steve's, her frame is always tilted in the morning. A legendary party animal, his framed self-portrait at Great Zimbabwe jiggles against the wall with excitement the minute guests even start peeking their noses into the dining room. As does the frame

My grandmother Ess aged 85

of Melea Letsoalo, our former domestic worker, who is captured in black and white, sporting a smile and a cheerful *doek*, about to sniff a pinch of snuff.

There are many photographs of Ess looking beautiful with high cheekbones and a sly smile, but my favourite is a black and white close-up portrait that Steven took of her when she was eighty-something. She is wrinkled and grey, but still beautiful and wicked, with a glass of wine in her hand, a steel clip in her hair and that persistently ungovernable twinkle in her eye.

There is also a picture of Jonah, who was Hatry the driver's son. He lived at Kings Walden until a few years ago, in a small room beyond the Italian Garden, alongside a chicken run and a long drop. There he grew some of the finest marijuana this side of the Limpopo, which came to be known in our circles as Jonah's Magic since a mere puff or two instantly rendered the user giggling, dribbling, glazed-eyed and helpless. There is also a photograph of Piers the Malawian mower and his family, sitting barefoot outside their hut, southern style, all serious and slave-like.

Of course there are lots of photographs of my lively mother, ranging from formal portraits of her playing the violin as a young girl, to one of her lying drunkenly on her back on the lawn with a chicken in each hand. One of my favourite photographs is of my father David wearing Buddy Holly style glasses and an undergrad look. His full name is David Atherstone Hilton-Barber and I've decided it's the second most stuffy after Kincaid Blatherwick, who lies in the cemetery at the top of the hill and whose exact connection to me I have never quite managed to work out.

The ancestral wall features a delightful photograph too of my older brother Brett, sporting sunglasses, a leather hat and the kind of insincere smile we all felt epitomised our notion of a seriously cool, agri-Mafioso type. He is standing behind a fruit stall with his business partner in the early eighties – he was dubbed Aubrey the Strawberry – and the sign on the stall reads: 'Ripe for Tonight' in

David Hilton-Barber at his graduation ceremony, 1956

reference, we can only assume, to the avocados they were trying to sell.

The photograph was taken in the early 1980s when they ran a fruit broking company called LSD, which stood for Lowveld Subtropical Distributors. The name of course brought a severe twitch to the *snor* of just about every right-wing khaki-clad farmer they ever dealt with. But as Brett pointed out, quoting the poet Roy Campbell, *snors* and beards were just about the only crop the Boers have ever grown without a government subsidy anyway.

My second cousin Mimi appears on the ancestral wall as a bonny young girl, dressed in tartan and lace, doing the Highland Fling in front of an amazed audience. She is captured in mid-air, a proud and delighted look upon her little face. My mother told me that Mimi farted like a pony the whole way through the dance, causing the judges to pronounce an early decision in her favour. Snuck into the collection is a postcard of a pre-colonial poor white European family – beleaguered father and mother and eight sad children on a tigerskin rug – which at a certain point in the evening Tana inevitably delights in telling people is our family in East Lithuania.

We are a mixed bag of descendants from English, Irish and Scottish blood, who arrived on these shores, and travelled and wandered, struck gold, founded towns, caused trouble, bred horses, farmed, gardened, loved like gypsies and drank like sailors. Shotgun marriages, extra-marital affairs, love across the colour line, untimely deaths, car crashes, shattered hearts, lost farms. The exhaustion of adventure represented on these walls is enough to drive anyone to drink.

My father's side of the family is woven into the tapestry through a series of photographs that include his parents Harold and Mary and his brothers and sisters on their wedding days, looking gorgeous and fresh-faced and far too young to even have sex; as well as a sprinkling of obscure relatives in jodhpurs and riding hats. His lot was bigger and chunkier, arriving as settlers in the Eastern Cape before heading out into the wild interiors, discovering gold in Barberton and prancing on all the way up to Rhodesia. The forebears of the Barbers weren't just raving adventurers, but clever to boot, like Ivan Mitford-Barberton, who sculpted the granite facade of the Union Buildings, and St Ledger, who started the *Cape Times*.

My father's ancestors Fred, Henry and Graham Barber discovered gold in Umvoti Creek in the De Kaap valley on 21 June 1884. They broke a bottle of gin over the reef, and named the place Barber's Camp. It later became Barberton, and there are still those in our family who grumble about the terrible waste of gin. Sometimes I think my mother's lot, the Tooleys, have been blamed unfairly for our family's wildness, but on the other hand, their line did introduce into the family a great love of lies, drama, drink and exaggeration. Take what a Tooley says, say the locals wisely, and divide by a hundred.

From both sides, the Hilton-Barbers – us and our Zimbabwean cousins – seem unfairly to have inherited not only a physical heaviness, but a bacchanalian love of the good life which has resulted in us becoming the bearers of heavy consciences and highly evolved super-livers that are practically big enough to go to school. We have also taken on a certain unkind pinkness of the skin that is entirely unsuited to the African climes, while our hair goes from surprisingly dark and fiercely curly to fine and pale blonde.

By some dint of genetic alchemy, the three of us children, Brett, Steven and I, inherited the same distinctive noses. Noses, as Steven always said, that were made for trouble. They are quite unlike anyone else's in the family and, frankly, defy classification. They're neither Roman, classical nor aquiline, but snouty, like ski-ramps with a flat tip at the end. My sister-in-law Josie says it looks like God pressed his finger under our noses when the putty was wet, and that he pressed the hardest on Steven's nose, the most flamboyantly upturned.

Family Hilton-Barber

We also inherited the same muscular calves – sturdy plump pink things – and sometimes I find myself gazing upon this wall of ancestors and wondering from whose loins exactly sprang this killer calf gene. Sadly, however, someone on my mother's side introduced weak knees, which I have inherited, along with one shorter leg and my father's predisposition towards sweaty feet. The uber-liver gene and a tendency to madness is scant consolation.

Tonight I sit sadly at the dining room table, all alone, letting the candle wax drip on to the table, thinking of all the dinner parties we've had here, of all the things that have happened, all the times that have passed. Tonight the photographs seem to me like the compound eye of an ancestral insect and I gaze upon them and wonder what the hell they've got in store for me next.

When the first bottle is done I head for the bar which, like the dining room, is filled with pictures – mainly from my father's side – and memorabilia like silver mugs presented by various godfathers, a few tennis trophies and of course an endless supply of alcohol. There is a framed picture of a poem that used to make Steven and me giggle. It says:

Come in the evening, come in the morning.
Come when you're looked for and come without warning.
A thousand welcomes you'll find here before you
And the oftener you come the more we'll adore you.

I had a small yellow radio in the shape of a snail and we would listen, torch in hand, to programmes on Springbok Radio, like Jet Jungle and The Mind of Tracy Dark and, on Fridays, the Springbok Hit Parade which ended at midnight with Number One. We never, ever made it to Number One, though, generally falling asleep around Number Seven, as DJ Gruesome Gresham implored us again to keep our feet on the ground and reach for the stars.

As I return to the dining room table from the bar my eyes fall upon a picture in the centre of the dresser. It is a picture of my brother

Steven and his son Benjamin and with the same strength of force as the day it happened, I feel the absolute shock I felt when my husband B opened the door from inside Steve's flat and looked me in the eye and said, 'He's gone, Bridge, he's gone,' and I realised that my brother was dead.

ℜ

'Bridgie, I can't get hold of Steven and he hasn't phoned ...' It was Monica, my sister-in-law, and she was calling from Maritzburg. She'd taken Benjamin down to her folks for the weekend. It was around eleven in the morning, an autumn day.

'He's probably busy,' I said absent-mindedly. It was a Saturday. I was in a sarong and T-shirt, making a lazy breakfast with friends on the stoep of our little Melville house. We were hungover, drinking Bloody Marys.

Two hours later she called again. 'I'm getting worried; it's not like him.'

'Maybe he's out of cellphone range,' I said, or something reassuring.

Then she called again.

'I'm worried, he normally calls first thing and then after Benjamin's nap and ...'

'Mon, are you sure you're not being paranoid?'

'I swear, I'm really worried.'

At about 4.30 in the afternoon I finally gave in her to nagging and B and I got in the car and drove over to their flat in Illovo. As we climbed the hill on Bolton Road, heading for Oxford Road, we saw the full yellow moon rising up into an orange sky, one of those brilliantly toxic acid-coloured sunsets for which Joburg winters are so legendary. My body flooded with adrenalin and I started shaking.

'Something's wrong,' I said, gripping my husband's hand. 'I know it.'

'Don't be silly, man,' said B, emphatically. 'Don't be ridiculous.'

'I can feel it, something's wrong, I know it.'

'You're panicking. Calm down, let's just get to the flat and find out what's going on.'

'I can feel it,' I said again. It felt like the ancestors had spoken in a moment with the moon.

We got to the flat and got the guard to let us in. Big glass doors opened into a fifties style reception area with polished floors and brass fittings; you know, those blocks that all the little old Jewish ladies have commandeered, organising themselves with complicated levy systems and infusing their apartments with the smell of strange cooking. We found the caretaker who didn't have a key to Steven and Monica's flat. We checked the parking. His car was there, locked. We went up to the third floor, and rang the neighbour's bell. They didn't have a key either.

'There's only one thing to do and that is to break in from the neighbour's balcony on to their balcony,' said B firmly. So we watched as he climbed on to the ledge of the neighbour's balcony, three floors up, and stepped carefully over on to the ledge next door. It was like watching Spiderman without the special effects, and my heart was banging and pounding so I went back to the passage and waited, staring at the flat door: a beige door with fluted frosted glass and a trellidor. Number 305.

And then B opened the door from the inside and looked me in the eye and said, 'He's gone, Bridge, he's gone.' My brother was dead. He had died of a heart attack in his sleep. His eyes were closed. He was lying in bed on his back, wearing a T-shirt that said: *In Your Eye*. And his bare feet had turned blue. I remember the television blaring and the curtains flapping and how I went into instant shock, and started jiggling like a marionette. My ears were roaring inside, everything slowed down and sped up again. Sounds faded and intensified.

I remember that I stood outside the flat when I called my brother Brett. The phone went on to an answering machine and then he interrupted, brusquely.

'Hi, Brett speaking.'

'Brett, it's me. Bridge.'

'Hi cupcake. Listen this isn't a great time, can I call you back in a mo ...'

'Brett, Steven's dead.'

'Ohmigod.'

That's all I recall of the conversation. I dialled Monica's number, but as I started speaking my voice strangled and choked and I gave the phone to B. 'Monica, Stevie's dead,' he said and started crying. And then everything descended into surrealism. I was given very sweet tea and what seemed like handfuls of tranquillisers. There were phone calls, the police arrived, friends, my mother's voice on the end of the phone saying over and over, 'He's not really dead, is he? He's not really dead, is he?'

The room filled with people, more friends, more curious neighbours. I sat in an armchair, shaking and drinking tea. The phone was ringing and ringing and B was trying to get medical aid numbers and cope with a flurry of calls from mortuaries and ambulance services that all seemed to want to offer a better price. Then eventually two guys in vaguely medical uniforms arrived, wrapped my brother up like a post office parcel and wheeled him off into the inky Johannesburg night.

The funeral was in Joburg, at Doves in Braamfontein. He was a photographer, part of that eighties crowd that chased the news around the country, from popular uprising to negotiated settlement to urban madness. He had worked along with Kevin Carter, Ken Oosterbroek (he married Ken's widow Monica), Paul Weinberg and others, a generation who saw the world change in front of their lenses, although his eye was arguably quirkier than most. Crowds filled the seats downstairs and the galleries upstairs and flowed on to the pavements. There were flowers and tributes and tears and farewells. Steve's son Benjamin cried the whole way through. We had a wake at Xai Xai in Melville, a hip little bar where the drinks flowed and everyone drank heartily and wept.

A few days later we had a smaller ceremony in the gardens at Kings Walden. It was pouring with rain – very unusual for May – and overcast. As we gathered on the lawn, a great big sunbeam lit up the crowd and my father stepped forward, to address the people and began crying.

I read a poem, the same one I had read at the funeral, by W H Auden, called 'Funeral Blues' (from *Collected Shorter Poems 1927-1957*).

Stop all the clocks, cut off the telephone,
Prevent the dog from barking with a juicy bone,
Silence the pianos and with muffled drum
Bring out the coffin, let the mourners come.
Let aeroplanes circle moaning overhead
Scribbling on the sky the message He Is Dead
Put crêpe bows round the white necks of the public doves,
Let the traffic policemen wear black cotton gloves.
He was my North, my South, my East and West,
My working week and my Sunday rest,

My noon, my midnight, my talk, my song;
I thought that love would last forever: I was wrong.
The stars are not wanted now: put out every one;
Pack up the moon and dismantle the sun;
Pour away the ocean and sweep up the wood.
For nothing now can ever come to any good.

The whole garden became sad, the rain dripped off the leaves of the wild syringa on to people's shoulders, the wind blew and in the distance the thunder rumbled. Then the rain came in again as the ceremony ended and people tottered inside, a heartsore community that had seen one of their children taken.

I don't really remember much of the rest of it. Isn't it funny how we shut out the dark parts? I remember Benjamin crying at the Joburg funeral and Andrew saying to me: *I heard you wail when the coffin was lowered.*

'Oh, going through the things is the worst,' I can hear myself saying aloud, suddenly, to no one, standing all alone in the dining room tonight. A candle sputters and from behind her frame, a flicker of concern crosses my grandmother's young face. I feel my own face wobble and crumble, and from inside a great welling of grief, like peristalsis. I take the picture of Steven and Benjamin down from the wall and cradle it in my arms.

A few days after Steven died, after the funeral, Monica phoned, sobbing, barely able to speak. I was at friends, it was a Friday evening.

'Uh, ah, aaah …'

'What, what?' I expected to hear something terrible, even more terrible than what already was. They say grief does that to you.

'I found, fou …'

Eventually I extracted the fact that she found one of Steven's hairs on the pillow in their bedroom.

It was an unbearably sad and bizarre image. I mean, you don't think about things like whether you'll leave a few hairs lying around after you're dead, do you? Is that all that's left behind? The sound of sobbing on the phone struck a strange contrast to the social clatter of friends in the lounge. Drinks were being poured. Someone was telling someone about their E trip. *Jissus, broer, you won't believe how lekker it was, hey …*

Steven's death felt like an amputation. The hardest to grasp was the fact that he just wasn't there any more. It was an acute physical loss. I was haunted by images of his blue feet, of his body being wheeled out on a trolley. I had shocking, terrifying dreams of him having a heart attack and collapsing in front of me, of him coming in through the door. I had to delete his phone numbers in my book, on the cellphone, the sound of his voice on a recorded message on the answering machine.

I went back to work after a week. I'd landed a job as editor of an airline magazine and I threw myself at it, leaving before the light, returning after dark.

'Hi Bridget,' said the voice on the other end of the phone at work. It was a colleague who'd been out of town. 'I'm trying to get hold of Steve, can you give me his number …'

I was haunted and grey, moody. I no longer recognised myself in the mirror. My eyes changed, I was purple with grief, pale and puffy from the endless stream of tranquillisers, bottles of wine, sleeping pills, calming down pills, anything I could take to escape the sadness, but of course I never could.

Steven's six-month-old son Benjamin was both a source of great joy in the months that followed, and a constant reminder of the loss of his father. He looked like a small version of his father, from his smile to his legs. I spent time with him and Monica at the flat – oh the ghastly flat – bathing him, feeding him, playing with him. Or Monica would drop him with me and we'd walk in the park, swim in the pool at our place. We used to call Steven the Labrador because of his inability to pass even a puddle without jumping in, or at least dipping his shirt in and putting it back on, soaking wet. He called it Poor Man's Air Conditioner. Like his dad, Benjamin wriggled with delight at the sight of water, any water.

My best photograph of Benjamin was taken by his godfather Andrew Meintjes. It's a black and white showing a laughing Benjamin standing trouser-less and waving a hosepipe into the air; the water caught in mid-splash, his delight caught in his dimples. On Saturday mornings Benjamin was delivered to Andrew, who had been one of Steven's dearest friends, and was a curly-headed delight of a character who built cameras, took photographs, designed computer systems and loved gadgets and espresso.

Mostly we sauntered on Saturday mornings in the trendy streets of Parktown North, to some funky deli or espresso spot, pushing the pram along the broad pavements under the oaks and jacarandas, three Steven-orphans, huddling closely together as passing people cast passing Nuclear Family Glances at us: approval at the wholesome picture of curly-headed father, mother and child, little knowing our real circumstances.

'It's a weird thing,' I remember saying to Andrew, 'but my whole sense of concentration and time is all out of kilter since Stevie.'

He squeezed my hand.

'I'm scared of everything, I keep thinking something else is going to happen, I keep waiting ...'

'It's all part of the trauma, darlin',' he said philosophically, but I caught the tear in his eyes too, glinting in the sun, the steady buzz of a high street in the background.

'Oh, it's not very attractive to be in mourning,' said Andrew, re-arranging his tears. We stopped and patted and kissed Benjamin. Smiling Benjamin, blissfully unaware of our sadness and its nature. In our fug of grief and insanity, Andrew, Monica and I spent hours carefully comparing Benjamin to Steven. Andrew would drink coffee, I would be drinking wine, of course, and the grieving widow a spritzer with diet sprite.

'His bottom is definitely Steven's.'

'Oh yes, but he has his mother's dimples and eyes.'

'But look at those legs. I'm sorry, those are *soooooo* Steven calves.'

'And mine,' I add quickly.

'Do you think he'll have his dad's huge penis?' Monica says, suddenly giggling.

We developed a peculiar ability to laugh and cry together within the same minute, caught as we were in an emotional maelstrom, sucked into eddies, spat out by tides, dumped by side currents. We all got used to crying in front of each other. Tears sprang and flowed and welled and poured. Faces paled, reddened, puffed, contorted. And the sounds – choking sobs, primal wails, animal-like grunts, and those endless breathless, panting gasps that signalled an oncoming outburst.

Benjamin regarded our grievous outpourings with a mixture of concern and intrigue. He would tug at Monica's hair, pull my skirt, slap Andrew's knees. His distractions worked. One of us would inevitably go from crying to picking him up and trying to be happy again. Oh, how we adored that little boy. Everyone adored him. He had the same charismatic quality as his father, the same interest in things quirky. We observed his developments keenly: his first teeth, his bowel movements, his first words, his first wobbly steps, his recurrent delight in squishing sandwiches into his ears. He gave us something beautiful upon which to focus as we mourned the loss of his big, delightful father.

And then he died too.

He was given the wrong medication by a private Joburg hospital after a routine operation that resulted in an overdose. He was eighteen months old.

It was Andrew who phoned me that morning.

'Hey, my darling,' I began cheerfully. 'How's thi ...'

'Bridgie, Benjamin's dead,' he said and began to cry.

From within my belly I heard the start of a hideous animal sound that came out of my mouth in a ghastly wail.

'Oh, oh, oh, ooooooo ...'

·~

Oh, it's all too much. Tonight within these ancestral walls, I clutch the picture of Steven and Benjamin, sobbing like there is no tomorrow. There *is* no tomorrow. I let out great heaving shudders that shake my sternum. Hot tears drip on to the dark wooden table. The dogs gather anxiously at my feet, one of them jumps up and starts licking at my knees.

'My boys, my boys are gone!' I scream. 'I cannot bear it ...'

Chapter six

At dawn I awake in my bedroom, still holding the photograph of Steven and Benjamin. It is a perfect sunrise, calm and promising. I shake myself and my hideously sad and foggy head and go and smoke a cigarette under the dead tree overlooking the mountains that change every day. The first light is grey then it slowly becomes orange, like a blush, as if someone is saying sexy things to the sky. In the Lowveld below, night-time lights are still flickering, their light diluting with the daybreak, making an effect like a heat shimmer. It is an ancient view.

The dead tree is a giant bone-white bluegum, white because it is dead, struck by lightning some thirty years ago, but still standing in defiance against these ancient blue skies like an arboreal totem, an antenna connecting us to the ancestors. The dead tree can spark a kiss, soothe a fight, delight a child, avert a crisis and provide the prefect excuse for just *one* more bottle of wine. It presides over the garden, providing omens and bearing messages, and I've come to regard it as a natural mast conducting the ancestral cellular network, as it were, of all the spirits plugged in here.

Some of the old spirits live at the top of the farm avenue in the family cemetery, cared for by a gentle old *waterbessie* tree and a troop of vervet monkeys. But most of them live in this magnificent garden which has flourished in direct proportion to the amount of tragedy that has unfolded at our door. 'Oh darling,' Tana always says about Kings Walden, 'malaria, drought, death, madness, hailstorms, you name it ...' To which my father always quickly replies, 'Well, there's never been a suicide.'

The dead tree was brought out, alive, to South Africa by my grandfather Billo's first wife, Muriel Frances, who was something of an Australian mail order bride. She was the sister of a pair of brothers who lived at nearby Pigeonhole Farm, who thought Billo would approve of her pioneering form and pliant nature, and so she came over to marry him without ever having laid eyes upon him. Tana calls her Sight Unseen.

The official version is that Muriel died at thirty-four of a broken heart upon hearing news of the death of her first grandchild from malaria. But our family's long-time domestic worker Melea has a different story altogether, which she told me one night over a bottle of corrosively sweet champagne, her favourite. Melea explained that part of her duties as a maid to the first set of our colonial grandparents was to keep watch over goings-on in the bedroom, and that Muriel Frances died while making love to a neighbouring farmer. You could say she came and went at the same time, a cheeky relative once said.

But I think it is fitting that Muriel's tree should be the conductor of the garden spirits. There is a Venda myth that tells of a young woman who is married, without ever having seen her husband. Unlike our Muriel Frances, her husband turns out to be a python. Horrified at discovering her new husband's true identity, she flees the country. A terrible drought ensues as a result of the python mourning his loss, and is broken only when another young girl is offered up to him. Like all good African myths, the offering must be repeated annually to keep the python god satisfied. 'Pythons and beer we can easily do,' said my brother Brett philosophically when I told him of the myth, 'but we could have a problem finding a virgin these days.'

I could spend the rest of my life looking for elusive virgins in this garden, I think to myself. When Tana was twelve years old she was flung out of the bath when lightning hit the side of the farmhouse. It imparted to her a great love of lightning and an extraordinary ability to garden. Hers is the fiercest gardener's gift. In her magical pact with the Lion Gods and other personal deities, she has provided the design and layout, and nature has provided the other essential living ingredients to create a complex and astonishing monument to our ancestors that spans three acres, several generations and many wild stories.

'There is no other place so romantic and dramatic and inspiring,' said chi-chi interior magazine *House & Leisure* once about Kings Walden's garden. 'The dreaming heights of Kings Walden, its bold vistas, intimate rooms, secret paths and poetic detail, but most of all its extraordinary spirit, make it our most romantic garden of the decade.' As you can imagine, it had the garden club in a terrible twitter. The past hundred years of my family's antics here in Agatha have long provided juicy fare for local luncheons, bridge parties and extended family gatherings, but it is the garden clubs that remain, if you'll pardon the pun, the greenest with envy.

Since Kings Walden garden has been open to the public in the last decade or so, thousands have passed through its green gates, with some of the more ardent ones having to be flushed out of the bushes after dark. There have been foreign visitors, garden groups, Christian clubs, charity parties, local outings and the odd conservative *tannie* who shields her eyes as she walks past the bare-breasted sphinxes.

It's usually after hearing the explanation of the dead white tree that religious visitors to the garden enquire as to my parents' persuasion – a fateful mistake on their behalf. 'A group of Christians told me today that the garden was so beautiful it must have been the hand of God,' Tana says often, in gleeful tone. 'I told them I was inspired by a young Muslim and his sensuous philosophy.' The young Muslim was her Burmese cat Miselu, but the Christians didn't know that of course, and would shift uncomfortably at thought of Allah lurking in the garden they were sure was the work of their own blonde, benign God.

Tana is enormously fond of these little games with visitors. Many a local Christian has dropped to their knees and promised to save her soul after hearing of her detailed exploits in the garden with her various lovers. She takes exceptional pride in offending the Calvinist sensibilities of any local Afrikaners who cross her path, regarding them, like Ess did before her, as an altogether inferior species worthy of death by social disdain.

'I must warn you,' we'll hear her start up in her best Queen's English, welcoming a deeply parochial Afrikaner with a mullet haircut, 'you may come across a dark Buddhist gentleman in the garden ...' at which point we all flee for the drinks cupboard, while the local listens earnestly to warnings about the scantily clad Buddhists that lurk in the azaleas and wishes like hell he hadn't left his gun in the car.

Tana never seems to tire of shocking people, and has used the same jokes again and again to great effect, much to our irritation. But despite her consistent protests and contempt for the many thousands of visitors who have passed through these delightful grounds, there are few who disagree that there are supernatural forces at work here – here, in the garden of my ancestors.

From the dead tree I walk across the lawns next to the swimming pool, and take a flight of wide stone steps that lead through an acre of purple agapanthus to a low ornamental lake called the Bibigar. 'Women spirits,' said Tana mysteriously when I asked her what it meant. The name was taken from Paul Scott's *Raj Quartet*, and this part of the garden has long held a semi-biblical status. The completion of the Bibigar was marked with the smashing of a champagne bottle, empty of course, the release of a flock of Chinese geese and the installation of two giant female sphinxes whose concrete nipples it is now deemed essential to rub for good luck.

The Bibigar used to be an old tennis court and clubhouse, which was ripped up by Tana to give way to this scene of poetic contemplation. When I stand at the rim of the waters and look out across the shimmering Lowveld I feel my solar plexus turn. It's a dizzying outlook, intersected by a fountain and two filigree cypress trees, black and lacy in the orange dawn, Moorish at sunset. A view that makes you feel anything could happen, anything wonderful and utterly unexpected. The ducks and geese that live at the Bibigar also like to stand out here at the water's edge as if they, too, are bewitched by this delicious sense of possibility.

Like ours, I guess, their lives have also been soap operatic, theirs resembling the domestic waterfowl version of *Days of Our Lives.* An extraordinary assortment of Chinese and Egyptian geese, peacocks, white-faced whistling ducks and more have lived, mated, bred on these shores, with most ending up in the slavering chops of lynxes, civets and badgers. Once there was a clever crowd of ducks that moved up to the swimming pool, sliding gracefully in as visitors arrived, as if choreographed by a ballet teacher hidden in a tree somewhere. But they drove my father mad and he drove them down the steps again, back into the jaws of fate.

At sunrise, when the skies and water meet, the female spirits of the Bibigar are awoken by soft peach kisses. At nightfall they are stroked to sleep by long cool shadows. This is a gentle place whose rocks and soil cover the secrets of other women spirits who also came here to admire the view long before we invented gin and tonic. The decorated pottery shards, Iron Age implements and smelting furnaces that have been unearthed in these Agatha hills attest to the antiquity of people who have passed this way.

Steven aged four or five

Not many visitors notice Mama Gidjane gently sweeping the moss-clad bricks alongside the Bibigar, in the shade of an old *mnali* tree. Her broom is fashioned out of the branches of a magic guarri bush, and she smiles a gnarled and toothless grin. Even fewer know that this humble, simply dressed woman is a *sangoma*, a traditional healer, the only indication a string of coloured beads around her neck.

Mama Gidjane has worked in the garden for as long as I remember, and loves to imbibe the Bibigar's female energy. She feels the earth's vibrations beneath her feet, she listens to the soothing coo-coo of doves in the *mnali* tree. She draws on the power of the dark, calm pools and entangled foliage. She drinks the rainwater collected in the bromeliads, their openings like red cowrie shells, and watches the white-bonneted St Joseph's lilies nodding yes, yes, yes.

My father can never understand why Mama Gidjane is always sweeping round the Bibigar, not knowing that for her it's like going down to the watering hole for a good old chat with all the ancestral sisters – her mother, my granny, her two sisters, Sarah. Mama Gidjane leaves little spirit SMSs for them – a pile of round stones, a stick, a nest – tucking them carefully amongst the gargoyles, spitting mythological beasts, plaques and statues that decorate the garden. Like Melea's, Mama Gidjane's ancestors are also buried close by, on the Solomons' farm next door, and they used to go there every Easter to pay their respects and take comfort in the cool eternity of the stones.

From the Bibigar, I follow a little path through the undergrowth to Steven's and Benjamin's Garden, a white garden, with camellias, azaleas, irises, plumbago and a goat fountain that spits into an old stone basin lined with decorative painted tiles. This was chosen as Steven's place of remembrance because the garden workers said the goat fountain reminded them of him. In the centre of the white garden is a sundial, a symbol, I guess, of the healing power of time, although now it seems only mocking.

I sit down on a concrete bench next to Steven's fountain. The camellias are in their final flower and some of them have fallen, like garden poetry, into the fountain. They look as if they have been sewn by hand, by a little old Jewish dress designer wearing big spectacles. They are stitched with such care and precision, almost invisible, each whorl arranged in perfect relation to the next. I imagine her sitting in a faintly lit parlour somewhere, in a wingback chair with her hair pulled back into a sensible chignon, glasses on her nose and the metronomic tick-tick of needle against thimble.

The azaleas are budding, the zebra grass is white and green, and the iceberg roses are starting to flower. I am flooded with unbearable pain. It's been nearly three years since Steven died and I still feel orphaned. I don't have a bigger, braver, wilder hand to hold any more. His was the one that held mine on the first day of nursery school, the first day of primary school, high school and university. His was the hand that held mine when I cried, laughed, fought and lived. When he died I lost my sense of safety, my friend, my confidant ...

Through my haze of tears I suddenly notice that Dr Zambuk, the Siamese cat, has followed me here and is rubbing up against the sundial, as if in deference to a special cat calendar. I manage a teary smile, and then something else catches my attention out of the corner of my eye and I see that behind the furthest roses stands a bushbuck. We hold eye contact for what seems like minutes and then, with a toss of her head, she disappears into the orchards below.

Her presence has moved me, and I get up and walk back to the house.

Steven, and Bridget aged three

Chapter seven

The next day I am called to the phone by Joyce. 'It's Melea,' she says.

'What's wrong, *mogadibo*?' (darling) asks the voice on the other end of the line and the sound of that cheery, crackly Sotho accent makes me burst into tears all over again.

'I'm coming to fetch you,' I sob.

So I hop into Black Beauty, an ageing BMW, and drive off towards Lenyenye, which is a rural township outside Tzaneen, to fetch our old family domestic worker, my *mogadibo*. She's over ninety now, and has halved in size and weight in the last few years, but remains a major source of comfort and a fine source of unexpurgated ancestral information for which she exacts payment in the form of sweet champagne, bags of mielie meal, linen, blankets and cash. Nothing for *mahala,* she says, nothing for nothing.

Bridget and Melea

I drive along what is called the Old Coach Road, now a badly patched tar road that winds down past the Coach House, where my granny first arrived, and corkscrews its way down into the steaming Letsitele Valley. The views are amazing: neat rows of citrus and macadamia plantations, the dam that was built by my second cousin's husband Mike Amm, the farmhouses in which they used to live – before the Land Claims – and the workers' compounds for the Coach House that are slightly Cape Dutch in flavour and are called Soweto and White City. Beyond, the charming chaos of distant rural settlements, puffs of woodsmoke and metal roofs glinting in the sun.

It's a glorious and mild day and I can't wait to see Melea again. I have known her all my life, and her family's lives and mine are so intertwined we're practically related. She raised my mother and her cousins, she raised us three children. She was there the night my grandfather died. She says a wild storm broke out – *medumo le magadima!* (lightning and thunder) – thrashing the skies and rattling the windows, and that my grandmother left his body lying in its coffin on the lawn, and drank Scotch until daybreak. There are always wild storms in her stories. When my grandmother died, some forty years later, Melea was there at her bedside too. Melea was born on Kings Walden. Her own parents were born in the area, and are buried on the Solomons' farm next door. She used to go there every Easter to pay her respects, before she became an old *mokgekolo*.

Melea lived with us in Craighall Park for some seventeen years, staying in the servants' quarters, a poky little room that shared a communal bathroom with whichever Garden Boy happened to be employed at the time. She raised me and my two brothers, saw us go from unruly toddlers to seventies schoolchildren, banner-waving university liberals to young people apparently incapable of holding down a steady job. Her eldest cousin Solly was our Garden Boy for a while, and in one of the family albums is a photograph of him in a starched white 'houseboy' outfit trimmed with red piping, and Steve, chubby and in rompers streaked with chocolate cake, a mixing bowl between them, big smiles on their faces.

Solly was a delightful character. His spell as Garden Boy was excellent for Steven and me, since part of his job was to pull us to Mrs Harper's nursery school on a little cart in which we sat on cushions covered in shwe-shwe fabric. The nursery school was only about three blocks from home, but Solly's routes were endlessly varied and interesting.

Sometimes we stopped at the Greek-owned café at the top of Bompas Road, and he would park us outside and go and chat to his friends, have a couple of roll-ups and take a few generous slugs from the nip that was going around. Sometimes we visited other domestic workers in their rooms, going in through the back gates and side entrances of suburban homes; other times we went via the park, stopping under the willows. One of our favourite expeditions was to a nearby café mysteriously named Rosebank Horsemeat Supply, where once again Solly chatted amiably to everyone, including the bald-headed owner who wore a grey dustcoat, and once again small bottles in brown paper bags exchanged hands.

I last saw Solly about three years ago at a braai at Melea's place. He was old and thin then – and died some months later – but still managed to gum his way through an entire T-bone steak – he had no teeth – and knocked back several beers and a few glasses of Hot Stuff. 'Crigell Puk,' he said drunkenly. '*Eish*, we had a good time there.'

At the bottom of the valley, I turn right at the T-junction towards Lenyenye, past Nkowankowa, which is the major township here, and extends into smaller ones like Dan, Kujhwana, Mhlaba Cross, Lenyenye and Tickyline that lie in the foothills of the northern Drakensberg. In Melea's parents' time, this area was practically uninhabited. Today there are spaza shops, car repair outfits, prefab cellphone stores, government billboards, roadside hawkers, schoolchildren, taxis, buses, goats, chickens and home-made, hand-painted signs that say things like: *Sheep Ahead*; *Pumpkins*

8kms; and *Mr Sharp Exhaust and Body Parts*. I pass the Tsunami Car Wash and Hair Salon – I imagine a bucket of water being thrown over my head and my car at the same time – and as I turn into Lenyenye, there is a big sign that says: *Tickyline Tombstones. Only R1 499 including erections.*

The sight of a blonde with sunglasses in a black BMW is strangely welcomed in the streets of Lenyenye. People shout and wave and stare, and I drive carefully along Stadium Drive, avoiding the chassis-busting humps and potholes, until at last I go right into Dirapeng Street, turn left into an unmarked side road, and pull up outside Melea's little house.

There she stands, tiny and smiley, framed in the doorway at the back of the stoep that is shaded by an enormous tree. I rush to hold this dear old woman in my arms. '*Jona, jona, jona joo ...* you won't believe what happened to me,' I say, tears welling up again, which they do with alarming frequency these days.

She makes me tea and cooks me scrambled eggs and I tell her about the robbery. '*Jona jona jona joooo ...*' she keeps saying too, and puts her hands against her ears as if expecting a loud noise. I act out an animated version of event – a flourish of a gun, my hands being tied, my heart banging against my shirt. She clutches her face, rolls her eyes, looks suitably aghast. '*Jo, mogadibo,*' says Melea with tears in her eyes. 'Don't worry, God will look after you.' And I go and sit in her lounge and smoke yet another cigarette while she goes and packs.

Inspired by the ancestral dining room at Kings Walden, the walls in her lounge are covered with photographs of her family and ours, except they are simply stuck on with Prestik and not framed. There are about a hundred pictures of assorted daughters, sons, relatives, weddings and funerals. There is one of Steve alive, next to one of his gravestone; me on my wedding day; a young Brett with her nephew Debele. There is a cut-out newspaper photograph of Madiba and Graça kissing on their wedding day, and one of Helen Suzman who

Melea and Brett

Melea mistakenly believes is my other granny Mary.

There is also a huge colour portrait of a chubby cheeked white man called Fernandez who has faded now to tea-coloured sepia. He was Portuguese and came from what was then Lourenço Marques to be foreman at Kings Walden. A combination of his Mediterranean lust for life, his warm and inquisitive presence, and the conducive surroundings, led him shortly into the arms of the beautiful young Melea Letsoalo.

In 1935 Fernandez supervised the building of a worker's cottage called Stone Cottage into which he and Melea moved. It had a modest view and was within walking distance of Kings Walden, but had no bathroom or electricity. My grandfather did not believe workers needed such luxuries. Melea and Fernandez appeared to care not, however, and lived there for some thirteen years, raising two boys and a girl, as nasturtiums grew wildly about the cottage and the three tall camphor trees in the front grew bigger and stronger.

Until one night in 1948, when there was a loud bang on the door in the middle of the night.

'*Maak oop, maak oop!*'

'Who's there?' Fernandez called out sleepily.

'*Maak oop, dis die polisie.*'

Fernandez and Melea were arrested under the recently legislated Immorality Act which forbade love across the colour line. They were tossed unceremoniously into the back of a police van and held in the Tzaneen police station for two days until my grandmother bailed them out and paid a large fine.

'I have never heard of anything more ridiculous in my life,' she said to the station commander, refusing to speak Afrikaans.

They were arrested twice more before Ess built a simple wattle and daub *rondavel* nearby for Melea to live in, and they dubbed it Fernandez Hideaway. It was struck by lightning ages ago, and has crumbled to the ground now. Melea and Fernandez remained lovers until his death in the late seventies. He is buried in the Tzaneen cemetery.

'One day we'll go there,' Melea always says. She is ready now with her bags and walking stick and we stroll slowly out to the car and drive back to Kings Walden.

Melea loves visiting. She walks around with the proprietary air of an important old *gugu*. 'When Billo was here it was the best farm,' she says to me, and then to the dogs who are lying in the lounge: 'What's the matter, dogs, are you drunk?' Joyce makes Melea pap and chicken wings and I open a bottle of red wine. Our interaction is a peculiar one. I return to being the baby child, she the comforter and imparter of universal wisdom. Our conversation turns on the fulcrum of her and my families, our various dogs and cats and, increasingly, the past.

'*Jo*, we had a nice time in 12 Northumberland,' she says as I light a cigarette and pour another glass of red. 'I used to drink and smoke,' she adds, approvingly. '*Jo*, I drank lots and I would fall down. I would take the taxi to Soweto with Rosina – remember Rosina? – and we would go to shebeens and parties and I would drink. Drink!' She claps her hands. 'And lose my umbrella.' She is laughing now, pretending to fall about drunkenly.

'What about Fernandez?' I ask her suddenly.

'*Jo*, he was a good man,' she says wistfully. I vaguely remember his visits, and the sharp stirrings of embarrassment as his large white frame darkened the doorway of the servants' quarters. But it didn't seem to bother anyone else much, and the sounds of laughter and clinking bottles went on well into the night. Steven was especially intrigued by the goings-on in the servants' quarters.

From the road, a wooden door opened on to a long bamboo-lined alleyway that also led to their rooms, and was also used by the Stapelbergs' servants at Number 10. They were a sorry pair called Lena and Phiri and they were hopeless drunks. According to Melea, Lena sometimes drank meths (methylated spirits) which would result in her weeping and howling in the alleyway like a crazed feral. Everyone beat up Lena. Phiri, Mr Stapelberg, his son Andre. Even Melea says she gave her a slap once.

'*Jo jo jo*, we had a nice time in Northumberland,' she keeps saying. And then she tells me about another white man who used to visit after Fernandez died, who worked for the airlines.

'His job was to clean the planes,' she says, 'and he would bring me all the things he found on the floor. Clothes, wallets, jerseys, bags …'

'What about *tatago* (father) and mama?' I ask.

'I told them he was a friend of Mickey (her son). This one came in a white car at night and we sat on the road and drank wine and opened all the presents. *Jo*, we had a nice time.'

The next morning my old *mogadibo* and I take a slow walk around the garden and down to the sunken garden, where there is a bench for her daughter Carol, who died of a stroke when she was about forty. She was a so-called coloured, and lived with relatives of Melea's for her early years. We sit awhile, she thinking about Carol and me thinking about the pool that is the centrepiece of the garden, where my grandmother used to swim in an ochre full piece costume with foam rubber cups.

The pool is surrounded by a circle of tree ferns that shade and slice the subtropical light. There are clivias, a purple lasiandra tree, moss growing on the little bench, which is guarded by a lion. In Thathe Vondo, a holy forest in Venda, the ancestral spirits are protected by a supernatural lion, Nthathe. It is no coincidence that lions, too, guard Kings Walden. Pools and lawns are watched over by an assortment of concrete lions in various conditions of age and erosion.

Some remain proud and defined, sporting Greco-Roman detail, other have weathered and eroded and resemble early African totemic art. They guard the entrance to the gardens, flank columns, sit upon pillars and spit from fountains. Tucked under creepers outside my father's office there is a lion's head with a sphincter-like mouth, round and crude and wrinkled.

Like the holy forests in Venda mythology, these gardens too have taken on the spirit of all who have lived, worked and toiled here, all who have swept and planted and weeded. Alongside the arches, steps and paved paths, builders and gardeners have signed their work, awkward inscriptions in concrete – Victor 1973; Johannes Miselu 2003; Frans Malatji 1988; Elias Malesa 2004. Mondays are *babalaas* days, when the gang is still giddy from the weekend's drinking, and the garden takes on a Shakespearean air as the staff fall about, Caliban-like, quarrelling, staggering and bumping into mirrors and statues.

I sit next to my old nanny for a while, holding her minute frame. And then I see, always with faint shock, the tattoo on the inside of her left forearm. It was enormously fascinating to me as a child, and I would rub it and trace with my baby fingers the outline of her initials – ML – in cursive Victorian script. The tattoo was very sore, she said. It was done by the boss of a citrus farm in Letsitele where she once worked. He had all his staff tattooed so that if they ran away they could be identified and returned to him. I always ask: 'What did you do?' And she always replies: 'I ran away.'

We carry on our wanderings through the garden, stopping to talk about various relatives and ancestors, and we visit the white garden and Steven's fountain.

'How is Andrew?' asks Melea, about Benjamin's godfather. And in a terrible instant I realise she doesn't know.

'He's dead too,' I say, and take her tiny black hand and squeeze it in mine as the tears start pouring down my face again.

'He's dead?' she repeats.

'Oh, *mogadibo*.'

And I explain how a year after Benjamin died I got a phone call one Monday morning from my cousin Helen.

'Bridgie,' she said flatly, 'Andrew was murdered last night.'

He was in his studio in Braamfontein when three armed men were let into the building under the pretext of making a delivery. They threatened to kill him and tied him up. As he lay face down on the floor he said, *Fuck, you guys won't kill me*. One stepped forward and shot him three times in the back. Nothing was stolen.

I'm at a point, sitting here in the white garden, where I barely have enough emotional energy even to feel sadness any more. It was the third funeral in three years. A harrowing gathering in the rose gardens of Emmarentia. Journalists, photographers, artists, friends, family. The Reverend Ron Nicolson, Monica's father, did the service. I stared at the crowd, numbed and beleaguered. The father, the son and now the godfather. My unholy trinity of tragedy.

'Sh, sh, sh,' says Melea. 'Don't worry, he is sleeping nicely in the ground.'

'So is your daughter Carol,' I say resignedly. 'Perhaps they'll have tea together.'

'Oh yes, they will,' she says.

Eventually Melea and I get up, walk slowly up the steps out of the sunken garden, steps that are charmingly tiled in blue. We go and sit at one of the tables overlooking the viewpoint and gaze out across the mountains, the glorious immutable mountains that have divided and united people like the Letsoalos and Tooleys over the years. While my lot pulled in with their guns and took the best bits of land, Melea's people were killed, imprisoned, and thoroughly dispossessed of their land following the Boer-Makgoba wars in the late 1880s.

'There's Mmamathola,' she says, pointing to an area above the Letsitele valley, where her parents lived until they were forcibly removed in the late 1950s. On 12 December 1957 an Order in Council, signed by the new Prime Minister Hendrik Verwoerd, was issued to Chief Malesela Letsoalo of the Mmamathola community, that 'in the public interest' they be removed to the farms Metz and Enable, a combined area of only 7000 hectares. The order listed the names of the tribespeople, over a hundred of whom carried the surname Letsoalo.

Some five hundred people had been living at Mmamathola since the century's turn, farming in the mountains above the fertile valleys where white farmers had settled. The white farms were irrigated by a canal taken out of the main river just below the Mmamathola community, and complaints by the farmers about the alleged degradation of their water source, the proximity of black people and their unrestricted movement across the farms, led to their eventual removal.

Melea was there the day when the police and army arrived.

She was also there, in full regalia, when Minister of Agriculture and Land Affairs Thoko Didiza officially handed over to the Letsoalo people some 1900 hectares of prime agricultural land in the Letsitele Valley in February 2001. She wore a bright headdress, a traditional cloth over a long sleeved shirt and a long black skirt, beads, bracelets, earrings, nail polish. It was hailed as a historic land claim settlement and cost the government some R3.5 million, although it has been racked by controversy and shenanigans ever since. Melea heckled from near the front, according to one of my cousins whose farm was handed over as part of the deal. 'You're lying,' she shouted out in Sotho. 'The government always lies.'

We look a while longer at the mountains and then she says to me: 'Don't cry when I'm dead; I will sleep nicely in the ground.' We walk back towards the house. The dead tree is almost fluorescent white, the sun shining down on its bone white branches. And then I notice the enormous Australian syringa tree next to it, the one that was brought out here by Muriel, has developed a huge crack down the middle.

'Look at this,' I say to Melea.

'Jo na mawe, watseba wena' (Gosh, you know), she says, putting her hands on her hips in that drama queen way of hers, *'Diphetogo di etla, diphetogo di etla.'* Change is coming, change is coming.

Chapter eight

When my parents return, the house becomes filled with gloom. We are all waiting for The Day, the impending third anniversary of my brother's death, and though we are trying to be cheerful, our silences are long and thoughtful. Sadness sneaks into the cupboards, pain creaks in the floorboards and door jambs. Clouds scud across the skies at funereal pace and, as if to underline the schisms of pain, the split in the syringa tree has worsened considerably.

I wake up on the day and it feels like my legs are on fire. My knees are burning, my calves cramped, ankles tight and aching. I can barely walk. I burst into tears, and somehow this breaks the ghastliness of the day and we all lapse into weeping and hugs and embraces and my father, my stoic father, drives me down to Tzaneen to Gail the physiotherapist. She tells me I have a condition called Restless Legs, which basically means post-traumatic stress. With every touch, she goes tsk, tsk, tsk like a mother hen, and shakes her head and looks sad and sympathetic. She knows my pain. She was at my parents' house when Brett phoned with the news that

Steven had died.

'You are toxic too,' she says. 'Stop drinking so much and smoking that stuff.'

Back at Kings Walden it is a snippy blustery winter's day, although the sun is shining and the garden is full of day visitors, who thankfully are dashing about the Bibigar and lower reaches of the garden since my father has placed a modest handwritten sign on a pot beneath the syringa tree that says: *Please do not stand under this tree, it may fall down*. The wind carries streaks of their laughter and chatter, which resound in awful contrast to our solemn mood.

Instead of lunching in the main dining room – all those pictures and reminders – we decide to dine quietly and cosily in my father's study. A fire has been lit, a table set for three, and we squash ourselves in amongst the books, the TV tables, the Dalmatians and Dr Zambuk. It is our favourite room, the most reassuring, and with the best mountain views from three windows.

The first course is a comforting country soup with fresh bread. We eat dispiritedly. Then in the middle of the second course, avocado with soy sauce and pecan nuts, both Dalmatians suddenly start from their deep, farty sleeps and sit up, alert. One leaps up and starts barking loudly, the other begins a low growl. Dr Zambuk also wakes up suddenly from where he was fast asleep, curled up like an anchovy. He starts miaowing in a raspy monotone.

'What is it? Dave?' my mother asks, in that voice. That worried voice. I hear the sound of wine being swallowed.

'I don't know,' he says, looking baffled.

Both dogs are barking fiercely now. Dr Zambuk is in full miaow.

I am peering over the rim of my wine glass, my preferred method of viewing the world these days, when there comes from the very heavens above, it seems, a great and horrible noise and I see the entire right-hand side of the syringa tree collapse and crash in slow motion against the low stone wall, sending up rocks and dust, like an explosion, before embedding itself half a metre into the lawn.

There is a long, exaggerated silence, broken in the end by the excited shrieks of the day visitors who have come running to see what on earth has happened. *'Kyk daar, kyk daar,'* says a young man with a two-tone khaki shirt and teardrop sunglasses. *'Ek kan dit nie glo nie,'* replies his wife, who is wearing a bright pink fleece. The tree is an angry red where the branch has split, and is bleeding great rivers of gummy sap. There is a pungent smell of fresh wood.

'Well, would you take a look at that,' exclaims a whiskered gent in a very English accent, pointing to the devastated lawn. And then above it all, I hear the clear and unmistakable sound of my mother's voice calling out to the waiter:

'Shadrack, champagne please!'

It is one of life's great delights to get thoroughly pissed with your parents. We put on a CD of the Mills Brothers and decide that the falling of the tree was a magnanimous gesture of greeting from Steve, wherever he may be, and we raise our glasses to him with renewed fervour and emotion. *'Glow, little glow worm, glow down yonder ...'* sings my father merrily along to the music.

'Oh, he was such a one ...' I slur, taking another great swig of red, white, whatever it was, 'but did we ever to stop to consider that maybe the fallen tree was the work of the ancestors of the initiation school?'

'Oooooooh,' says my mother with a twinkle, 'now there's a thought.'

My father coughs.

'Aah, the valley of the circumcision,' he says mysteriously. 'The place where things are forgotten.'

'Forgotten!' I splutter in delight, I've got champagne bubbles in my nose now. 'Would you care to remind us?'

'Well, once upon a time, I think it was in 1990,' he begins, 'I was approached by Patrick Letsoalo, Melea's son, to ask if he could hold an initiation school on the farm. He was an inspector with a transport company in Lebowa then, he must have been in his fifties ...'

As he talks, I look across the first valley into a green crotch of indigenous bush. Every year, in a secluded place, male Sotho adolescents undergo a secret and transforming process: their initiation training. They go in as boys and come out as men. No outsiders are allowed into the camp. This unassuming patch of Agatha bush was the place selected for that particular initiation school.

'I had to use four-wheel drive on the Jeep to get to the stream,' my father is saying, 'that flowed from a spring in the forest. Next day work started with the clearing of the undergrowth and the construction of a crude shelter out of poles and brush. I returned in the afternoon and gave Patrick the medication he had ordered – bottles of gentian violet, meths and antiseptic. And cotton wool and Minora blades. 'You can come along on Friday at – ' whatever time, Patrick indicated with his hands where the sun would be. 'But only you. I am going back now.'

We all shiver in anticipation in the cosy little fire-warmed study.

'When I arrived on the appointed day,' my father continues, 'there were some forty young boys, stripped and standing in a line in the dappled sunlight. They had been arranged in descending order of size and their bodies were covered with clay. I looked down the line of faces, nervousness here and there, but no real fear. Some of

Initiation photo taken by Steven in 1990

them returned my gaze coolly. I wasn't sure whether to greet them but at the word from Patrick, they all clapped. I held up my hands in acknowledgement.

'There was also a group of young men holding long thin canes and, of course, the elders. Then the singing started, a refrain repeated with vigour by the young men. Patrick led me down to the Doctor's Place and said they were about to begin. I stood back feeling conspicuous and incongruous. Magwela was there with his instrument and a tin holding a mixture of medications. With him were four men ...

'The first lad was led down the trail to the spot, his face covered with a cloth. His arms were gripped by Magwela's assistants and he was pushed, not roughly, into a sitting position. His legs were held apart and Magwela got to work. I watched the youth's face – he winced, then gave a terrible groan, he was finding it difficult to contain his cries. It took longer than I expected, the foreskin is removed ...'

'Stop!' shrieks my mother. 'Where was Steven all this time?'

'Where do you think?' replies my father. 'Taking photographs of course.' He sighs. 'When I left I felt like I was driving away from a bygone age.'

In my mind I can hear Steven's altogether more vivid descriptions of the month he spent photographing the initiation school. He was completely and utterly fascinated by the rituals, the boys, the elders, the motives, the meaning.

'Like, there's the stabbing of the elephant,' I hear him saying. Excitedly. 'It's a ritual at the fire, and then when the circumcision happens, the old men shout: *Sever, sever with the knife, let the fishes take.*' I can picture him making fish movements with his hands, and clutching at his crotch, as most men automatically do when the subject of circumcision comes up.

'The novices, the youngsters, they're known as cane rats, hey. And they run through a rank of singing men, and the ones that bleed a lot are meant to have fucked around. And the swearing, the swearing is all part of it. And these guys spend a whole month in the bush, naked, in the middle of winter ...' And then I think of the awe with which both my brother and father spoke about the final ceremony.

When the word was given, the boys started to advance slowly, bowed to the ground stretching out first one leg, then the other, emulating the gait of the chameleon, the creature that signifies wisdom and prudence. The procession shuffled forward raising a small cloud of dust. Shepherds ran in front, singing and beating their sticks on the ground. The old men walked along in the rear, maintaining their dignity. They disappeared into a grove of litchi trees to prepare for the symbolic farewell ceremony. They donned grass skirts and then emerged in small groups, holding their hands at the sides of their faces to perform the special dance with high jumps, while the shepherds ran swooping and whirling beside them.

They spent two nights awake, singing and dancing at the dam at the bottom of the farm. And then some of the elders slipped away to the camp and tore down the structures which, together with the grass mats and other paraphernalia, were piled up and burnt, the great conflagration consuming also all the filth and ignorance of childhood.

'Oh, those were my favourite photographs,' I hear Tana saying, her voice breaking my reverie. A selection of Steve's photographs of the initiation school were published in Sunday magazine under the editorship of Jenny Crwys-Williams in November 1990, at the same time as an exhibition of them opened at the Market Theatre in Johannesburg.

To say they caused controversy is an understatement. The news-papers, radio stations and TV programmes buzzed with debate. The photographs were torn off the walls at the Market Theatre and the workers went on strike. Somewhere – oh somewhere! – buried in one of my boxes I have a newspaper clipping of a front page pic of a striking worker with a placard saying: *Down with Steve Hilton-Barber.* Of which he was very proud.

Steve's photographs catapulted him into a different realm altogether, but I know he was deeply sensitive about them too. I remember being on holiday at Hunters Moon, Brett's house, that December, when there was a massive storm in the night, with wild lightning strikes. We were all woken by the sound of singing and Steve wouldn't let me go back to sleep. He was scared, he said, that they were coming to get him. 'Hey, it's the lightning, china,' I said comfortingly, but we waited until the singing and the rain and the darkness disappeared, and then he said he was going to walk down to the bush where the school had been held to ask for forgiveness.

When I woke up some time later, he was back on the stoep, cheerfully eating a hearty breakfast of scrambled eggs and bacon. 'What happened?' I asked sleepily. 'Oh I went down to the school and sat in silence,' he replied. 'And then I saw two purple-crested loeries mating in the tree and decided that I had been forgiven.' And then he lifted up a piece of bacon between two fingers, leaned his head back and dropped the bacon into his mouth.

Chapter nine

Like falling trees, hangovers tend to leave destruction in their wake. The morning greets me with a heavy head and heart. I have an appointment, booked by mother, agreed to reluctantly by me, with a trauma counsellor from Pretoria, who visits every fortnight, and whom the family doctor has apparently said is 'very good'.

'What do you mean "very good"?' I ask.

'Well, Dr Boon says he is very experienced in dealing with These Sort of Things.'

I succumb. I have after all, lost my brother, my nephew, a dear friend, been held at gunpoint and left my husband. Who knows, perhaps the unlikely sounding Koos may help.

I pull up outside the freshly built doctor's offices in town. It's definitely growing; there are houses being built all over, and For Sale signs are springing up like mushrooms. What is some Lowveld quack gonna tell me about life that I don't know already? I think, squashing my cigarette angrily in the car ashtray. Inside the waiting room there is a smartly dressed and anxious looking black woman and a miserable looking guy in a wheelchair with a plaster cast. Disinfectant hangs in the air like pointlessness.

I fill in a long form, pace around a bit, flip through a pile of health magazines. I hate them, all those glossy pictures of happy shiny people. Why don't they have magazines showing sick people? I wonder bitterly. Why don't they show photos of runny noses and suppurating wounds?

'Breed-jhurt?' asks a plump Afrikaans nurse with a remarkable bouffant hairdo. She is remarkably manicured too – eyebrows plucked, face flattened with base, eyeliner, lip gloss, brown to deepen the cheekbones, a parrot-like green above her eyes. I am wearing jeans and a T-shirt that both need washing. My heart is sinking like the Titanic. I allow myself to be led meekly into a small office with a brown carpet and government-style desk.

I realise my mistake the minute I lay eyes on Koos.

'Oh my dear,' he says, stepping forward to greet me.

He is in his late fifties, weather-beaten and conservative. *Verkramp.* He's wearing a pale green polyester shirt with sweat marks under the armpits, shiny grey suit pants and pale grey shoes. His glasses are thick, black-framed, strands of his black hair have been swept over the top of his balding pink pate and, call me streetwise, I know instantly that my interaction with Koos – in my mind he is already Koos the Doos – is going to be an absolute disaster.

'So you had an armed robbery, right?' He looks at me expectantly, shuffles his wire-bound feint and margin notebook and says: 'So how do you feel about them now?'

'About who?' I ask testily, and realise he means black people.

He coughs nervously.

'Look,' I start, 'this is not about what you think the blacks do.' Koos has instantly rubbed me up the wrong way, he's pushed the racism button and that's pushed my anger and contempt button. I launch into a full-on attack. 'This is about me being held up, at gunpoint, against my will, by some motherfucking criminals who don't give a shit about life,' I say. 'I've had a huge, enormous violation of my privacy, I have been held up – no, tied up, I have seen my husband tied up – except I've left him now, the stupid bastard – and my tenant tied up and fucked up and now you're fuckin' telling me … now you're trying to turn it into some kind of racist something …'

'Oh my dear,' he says, 'you are very angry!'

'Of course I'm angry!' I shout, thumping the table with my fist. 'Wouldn't you be if someone just walked, I mean, just walked into your fucking lounge and fucking held you up and said they were going to kill you and then they fucking tied you up and then took like every fucking thing you fucking owned …'

'Now, now,' says Koos, extending his hand across the desk. 'I understand you are cross. I have been a counsellor with the police for many years and I understand that you have been through a great deal …'

'The police?' I shout. 'What do the fucking police know about crime?'

And then the absurdity of the situation strikes, and I take a deep breath, sit back, slap my hands against my knees and say to Koos the Doos: 'I'm sorry, I'm stressed out, strung out, fucked up …'

'Right, my dear,' he says, seizing the moment and picking up his notebook with renewed enthusiasm, 'I want you to take a deep breath and picture a beautiful rose, a beautiful rose in your mother's garden …'

'How do you know about my mother's garden?' I ask suspiciously.

'Everyone here knows about your mother's garden,' he replies, in faux soothing tones. 'Now, picture the rose, maybe it is a deep red, perhaps it is orange or even a lovely pink.'

But all I can picture is the rose on my screensaver, which someone once said looked more like a vagina than a rose.

'It's not working,' I say after a bit.

'Oh my dear,' he says again. 'You are so very tense. Why don't you come back this afternoon? I can make another half hour for you and we can try again? What do you think?'

'This isn't going to work,' I reply. 'This is definitely not going to work!'

'Is there something else you'd like to tell me, dear?' he asks.

'Yes!' I shout. 'You're an idiot who thinks the police have a snowball's hope in hell of combating crime and not only have I been held up by a bunch of cunts but I've snorted cocaine, smoked dagga, lost my brother, lost my nephew, been locked in chookie by the fucking apartheid cops, had friends killed and now you think you can come along and tell me …'

I'm not sure if it's the mention of cocaine, dagga, death or apartheid, but Koos's eyes have widened considerably and from behind me I hear the anxious shuffle of the bouffant lady. I snatch my bag from the floor and stomp out of the room. 'Fuck you and the other motherfuckers,' I mutter as I flounce out the clinic. 'What a bunch of wankers …'

'Why don't you take a wander through the garden?' Tana says gently when I tell her about Koos the Doos.

'Shall I get you a bottle of wine?' asks my father helpfully.

My garden walks always start with visiting the Dead Tree but today, instead of heading down towards the Bibigar, I take a broad grassy path to the right and head up a flight of brick steps, past a sweep of purple plectranthus into the top garden. The start of the top garden is a paved lookout point decorated with a pair of Italian-style fountains – bare breasted women bearing a pool on their heads – and an ornamental concrete bench.

This is the Liquidation Bench, which commemorates the final loss of the farm to the Land Bank. By deliberately facing the very land which was lost, and the mountains behind, the Liquidation Bench is designed to provoke great remorse.

That is the soul of this garden, I guess. Every place evokes an emotion by marking an event, mourning a loss, celebrating an achievement, enshrining a cat. There is a garden of emotions in a little village called San Remigio in Italy.[3] The garden was designed by Sophie and Silvio Remigio, who both grew up in the mountains and settled there in 1883, designing a vast garden of terraces, each one designed to evoke a specific emotion. Sophie made a model of the garden which she placed in the moonlight to test out the effects. Plainly her model worked – and the garden was completed nearly forty years later.

The entrance drive winds through a park flanked with ash trees, azaleas and rhododendron. The bottom terrace is the *Giardino della Mestizia* – the Melancholy Garden – which has rectangular patches of lawn with wrought iron fences and worn stone lions and urns once filled with myrtle. In the far wall is a niche with a statue of Hercules and Hydra, alongside *nymphaea* – grottoes dedicated to nymphs.

The next level up is the *Giardino dei Sosperi* – the Garden of Sighs.

---

[3] Judith Chatfield, *The Classic Italian Garden*.

Here, stone benches invite contemplation and parterres with low box borders are planted with roses between paths set with *fleur de lis* pebble patterns. In the centre is a life-size sculpture of Venus on a large seashell driving her sea horses, and against the walls are niches with statues of a cavalier holding a sword and a lady in a farthingale, a shepherdess and Silenus, the wise tutor to Dionysus.

Two flights up one enters the next terrace through a stone arch covered with roses. This is *Giardino della Memoria* – Memory Garden – where statues of three putti dance in a rectangular flower bed. Once Sophie grew white roses here, trained in garlands, and red flowers spilled out of urns. A wrought iron gate leads to woods off the side and on either side steps lead up to the next terrace, the *Giardino delle Ore* – Garden of the Hours – whose central feature is a sundial and a statue gesturing for silence. An inscription says the sundial was placed there by Silvio and Sophie to mark the sunny hours brought on by the dawn, which drove away the shadows of the night. There are statues of Pluto, Venus, Bacchus and Juno.

The final terrace is the *hortus conclusus*, the enclosed garden, which is directly below the villa. The walls are covered in ivy and four columned niches are built into the retaining wall and decorated with patterns of dolphins and garlands. A yew is trimmed in the shape of an armchair, contrasting with four stone chairs formed by dolphins supporting seashells. Sophie's beloved roses continue to grow on this spot.

When I sit at the Liquidation Bench I picture my mother sitting here as an Italian widow, in a dramatic Italian film with badly spelt English subtitles. She is beautiful in black clothes, a lacy headdress. She weeps as she gazes out across the land on which she was born and which is no longer hers. 'Why did we farm the only fruit out of which you can't make alcohol?' she asks, looking at the camera. She is talking Italian of course, and the camera does a slow mournful pan across the lost farmlands and the mountains that change every day. 'Why did we have to have such bad luck,' she cries, 'drought, hailstorms, death, murder ...'

'But you still have a guest house and a garden,' pleads an elderly relative, also in black, and on bended knee. At which point Tana weeps even harder.

As if in sympathy, the sadly trickling fountains speed up their trickle. Poetically, one of the water bearers never gets her pale concrete face wet. Below Tana's feet are piles of empty bottles of *vinho verde* and red roses, and behind her three mandolin players with thin moustaches are singing a sad lament to the family dog who lies buried alongside the bench. His name was Zingwe, and his death involved heavy tranquillisers and a shotgun.

I get up and start walking slowly along a stone path towards my own garden of sighs. The path leads round an old reservoir with swathes of red salvia dancing around its belly. It is covered with an unruly bougainvillea. It used to hold the water for household use until a worker went in to clean it and nearly died from inhaling unusually high concentrations of Agatha algae.

Next to the reservoir stands an ancient lime tree, which deserves a prize for supplying limes for all G&Ts drunk over three generations, which in my family amounts to a modest river, say, like the Limpopo. Instead of being exhausted though, constant plucking, vigorous pruning and judicious watering have encouraged it to proliferate. And 'let's go get a lime' has been code for just about every kind of activity from a stolen kiss to smoking a joint.

Behind the reservoir is a run-down building called Sheep Shed, my childhood escape, my long-time sanctuary. Isn't it strange how I cling to the ruined parts as my garden of sighs and melancholy? My granny kept sheep here when we were young, and it was one of my and Steven's favourite playing places. It was also one of my mother's favourite playing places too, even though there were cows then. She once tried to do an impersonation of Mary Poppins and climbed on to the roof of Sheep Shed with an umbrella and jumped off and broke her leg.

Today it is a dusty and collapsed structure, sanctuary to lazy lizards and greedy weeds that peek through the cracks that smell like soil and worms. I remember when it was home to ten or so sheep that grazed greedily in the pasture by day and huddled in the shed together at night, counting each other to go to sleep, or whatever it was I imagined they did. I lie down on a blanket on the grass next to Sheep Shed, pour myself a glass of wine and let the breeze ruffle my furrowed brow. In the distance I can hear the teasing shriek of ravens, such a winter sound.

My friend Sam calls from Joburg. 'Hey, hey, what'ya doing, girl-friend?' she asks cheerily. I can hear the sound of an office in the background, clicking keyboards and the thrum of electronics.

'I'm lying on my back drinking wine next to Sheep Shed,' I say and she starts laughing.

'Sheep Shed?' she asks.

'It's an old ruined shed next to a lime tree under the bluegums looking on to the mountains,' I reply.

'You lucky fish, you lucky fucker. I'm stuck in an office in the middle of Hyde Park.' And then she says, 'But, so how are you really?' in that caring tone and I feel the tears well once again.

'I frankly don't know what the fuck I am going to do with myself, Sammy,' I warble pathetically. I sit up on the blanket, knocking over my glass of wine. 'Oh fuck! I mean, I can't go on living with my folks, getting pissed every day, consumed with pain and madness. I mean, I just feel wracked with grief, traumatised, I hate my stupid fuckin' ex and I miss my brother ...'

'Oh Bridgie,' she sighs.

I switch off my cellphone and spend the afternoon wailing and sobbing, slugging wine and thinking of all the times I spent here,

Mupi the 'houseboy' and Melea

at Sheep Shed, on the farm, with my grandmother, my brothers. We stayed on and off for weeks, sometimes months, becoming dangerously feral the longer we stayed. I was once left with Ess for six weeks and apparently didn't recognise my parents when they returned, sulkily refusing their gifts of charming cuckoo clocks and tartan skirts from Europe.

When they were there, our parents Entertained and our daily lives were managed through the Servants: Melea was imported from our home in Craighall Park, then there was Chief Houseboy Mupi and two maids called Mayede and Kodze. When did we start resorting to the Anglicised strings of Joyces and Emilys and Lizzies, I wonder. The Servants lived at the Compound, where Melea slept on a bed raised on bricks because of the tokoloshe. They ate their meals at Cook House, an open-walled, brick building with a fireplace in the middle.

A fire burned here all day long and the tin roof inside was blackened with smoke. While we dined on gourmet cuisine in the farmhouse, in Cook House we ate pap and *morogo* (wild spinach) with chili and peanuts, overcooked meat, blackened chicken wings, gizzards, innards, gristle, dripping bone marrow, sheep's eyeballs and cow's brains. They were delicious.

Sometimes we walked to the cemetery to say hello to the ancestors. Melea showed us how to put a small pebble in your mouth, swirl it around and spit it out on to the grave. I loved this ritual and did it several times, repeating after Melea 'Hello Billo Tooley' as we spat on to his grave and did an exaggerated wave and wiggle of the hips. '*Sala gabotse* (go well), Billo Tooley.' I did this ritual for my granny too, although I was in my twenties then.

During the week we walked to Doone Glen, where the farm water came from, to collect clay to make cows and things. Mupi made the best cows; in a series of deft pinches he fashioned Ngunis which we kept until they dried and crumbled or got thrown out. After our walk, Mayede or Kodze washed our feet in big tin tubs as we sat on the stoep. Sometimes Mupi carried my hobby horse, which was called Bess-a-Luck and made out of a stick and a stuffed sock.

For Steven and me it was a great honour to be allowed to go with Mupi to Sheep Shed and watch a sheep being slaughtered for the pot. 'Go along, go along,' my granny would say and we would each take one of Mupi's hands, which we let go of the instant we were out of the main gate and ran like hell up to Sheep Shed. Here, a group of workers gathered and after lengthy discussion, some poor unsuspecting creature was chosen. Two workers grabbed the feet of the sheep and bound them with wire, then flipped it over on to its back, then another quickly and skilfully slit its throat with an enormous knife that had been sharpened on a big rock nearby.

As its sticky red blood drained into a black pot (later spirited off to Cook House), its twitches slowed, its eyes rolled and flickered and its life ebbed warmly away. With a final shudder it died. Mupi skinned the sheep and slit open its stomach so we could see the slimy half-digested grass inside and its intestines in peach and purple coral colours, like strange sea creatures. It smelt like blood and grass and fat and stomach juice all mixed together. And how odd a sheep looked without its woolly coat, without its hooves or head. Steven was entirely unafraid of this sheepy, smelly flotsam and jetsam, and would poke around looking for bits with which to terrorise me.

When it was all done, the skin removed, the legs off, the meat chopped up, the delicacies apportioned, there was nothing but a dark stain on the grass, perhaps the odd hoof left lying about for the dogs. When I lay in bed at night I used to wonder if the other sheep could smell the bloody grass and if they knew what had happened ...

And then for some reason my mind flashes on to a photograph from one of the family albums. It is Christmas Day 1969. Steven and I have been given the most enormous black and white panda bears, and we are captured in celluloid alongside a black man in the brightly coloured gear of a traditional healer or *sangoma*.

Tana had invited him over on Christmas Day to come and bless the family and add a little paganism to the proceedings. His name was Dr Neverdie, and he came from Dan village, near Lenyenye. Despite his name, he died some years ago, and his first wife continues to sell muti and advice to locals and extort the odd cherry-faced tourist.

We all gathered on the patio outside the kitchen at drinks time, which was a generous 11.30am. Ess, Melea, Tana, Brett, Steven and my father. Dr Neverdie arrived to the gentle tinkles of ice in G&Ts, the waft of Chanel No 5 on the Agatha breeze, the clutch of pale faces shaded by an ancient *mnali* tree. He was bare-chested, with a real leopardskin slung over his shoulders, his ankles and wrists covered with beads and bangles and baubles, to which were attached little cowrie shells, mirrors, feathers and bones. On his head he wore feathers and sunglasses. He smelled of Zambuk and trading stores.

'Excellent day, thank you for visiting, doctor,' said Tana welcoming him on to the patio.

'*Dumela, thobela, awudzi,*' he announced cheerfully, and then with a great whoop and shake of his stick, he leapt forward and began chanting and crying out. '*Re kgopelele gore dillo tsa rena di kwewe ke badimo ea rena le moya wa Modimo o re ŝegofatŝe, rena le leselo le mo letŝatŝing le lebotse le.*' (We ask you, oh lion one, to hear the cries of our ancestors and we plead to the spirits of the Great One to bless this farm and to bless these people on this lovely day.)

My grandmother delicately adjusted her sunglasses and my mother took a sip of wine. Melea clapped and cried out: 'Bless us again, oh wise one, bless again and let us have many cows and children.'

'Oh wise and great one,' brayed Dr Neverdie, 'bless this lovely white family for they are good and bless the lovely young Letsoalo and her clan. Bless me too and let me feel you working the spirits and let me hear your message and blessing.'

He shook his stick and stamped his feet on the ground, leaping and whooping and jumping into the air with great agility. I inched behind my enormous panda whose eyes, too, seemed to have widened at the sight of Neverdie in full throttle. Steven took a step forward. Brett clutched Melea's hand.

'Oh wise one!' bellowed Neverdie. 'Oh great and beloved one!' His bangles tinkled and his beads and bottle tops rattled. Melea shook her hips and clapped her hands and Tana raised her glass and shouted 'Come along, Doctor' and Steven giggled. Neverdie pranced and danced and roared out like a beast. 'Oh wise one, great Nkosi!'

And then suddenly Dr Neverdie flung his stick down on to the ground and dropped to his knees and clutched his heart and pointed at Steven.

'*Mfana, ke pelo ya mosimanyana!*' he yelled. (The boy, his heart, his heart!) '*Badimo bare pelo ya gagwe ga e na kgotlelelo!*' (The ancestors say weak heart.)

'His heart,' said Melea translating, 'he says Steven has a weak heart.' We all looked at Steve who looked back with his wide brown eyes.

'Shall I go with Dad to get the wine?' ventured Brett, all of twelve years old and already well skilled in the art of oiling the family wheels.

It seems like aeons later that I emerge, soggy and disgruntled from Sheep Shed. A hot wind is whipping through the tops of the bluegum trees and the skies echo with the fading cries of hadedas, like pterodactyls as they fly homeward. I feel like I've been watching a Federico Fellini movie. The bottle is empty, the sun is going down. I am cold and *dronk verdriet* and shuffle across the lawns back to the house like an old hobo, blanket around my waist, hoping to avoid being seen.

'Oh, there you are, darling!' calls my mother. 'Guess what? You won't believe what's happened – Mr Schnitzel just phoned to say Stone Cottage is for sale, it's on the market, isn't that amazing?'

It takes a few seconds before it sinks in that Stone Cottage, the cottage next door, the property next door, the very one where Melea and Fernandez lived, is up for sale. And somehow I know in an instant that it will be mine.

The dead tree – struck by lightning the night my grandmother Ess died

Detail of the Italian garden overlooking the Agatha hills in the distance

The Elsie Tooley memorial fountain

Mabula in a pond - one of the many at Kings Walden

The entrance to Kings Walden

Mabula and Congo on a 'secret' path through the garden

Bust dedicated to my grandmother on my father's side, Mary Hilton-Barber

Detail of the Bibigar – originally part of the clubhouse and tennis court

The Billo Tooley fountain, dedicated to my grandfather

The path to the sunken garden

Brett, Christmas 1969

Steven and Benjamin, taken with a self-timer

Family lunch, my father and me, 2000

A family member's birthday, 1995 – Steven, Monica, Tana, Bridget, Brett and David

Chapter ten

It was in Stone Cottage that our ex-domestic, the young Melea Letsoalo shared her first shivering naked kiss with Fernandez the Portuguese foreman on my grandfather's farm. Melea had graduated then, from helping in the vegetable garden, to chief nanny in charge of looking after my mother and her cousins Mimi and Delia. She spent her days walking with the children in the gardens, going down to the vegetable patch, pointing out different things: flower, lettuce, monkey, frog.

Fernandez was a hearty happy man from Lourenço Marques whose Portuguese accent rolled off his tongue like butter off a prawn. He built the simple original structure of Stone Cottage: a long room with concrete floors and two low, deep windows. There was no bathroom or electricity, and outside he planted three camphor trees and some nasturtiums around the water tank. The weather in Agatha was deliciously mild compared to LM, where the air was salty and viscous. Billo Tooley, his new boss, was agreeable, organised, rich and, well, pretty pleasant all round. Fernandez liked him.

And he lusted after Melea. He lusted after her with such powerful, groin-aching lust it was practically impossible for him to concentrate in her presence. He had noticed her first in the Kings Walden kitchen with an older woman who he came to discover was Mama Gidjane, said to be a witchdoctor. His time with the locals in Moçambique had taught him that even if you didn't believe all that hocus-pocus – which he would eventually come to regard in an altogether different light – it was best to show respect.

The first thing he noticed about Melea was her eyes. Big soft, brown eyes, and when he deliberately caught her gaze, she looked straight back at him and smiled with a slight arch of the eyebrow, with a princess-like air of expectation, as if she expected him to address her with an important message or at least something suitably entertaining.

Fernandez put out his hand and addressed her in Shangaan, which he knew a little better than the local Sapedi, northern Sotho.

Thobela, he said. She offered her hand, and put the other one on the inside of her forearm, a traditional greeting in which both hands are displayed to show good intent and the fact that one was not concealing an assegai, for instance, or a sharpened stone.

He began seeking her out in the mornings after his briefing with the boss, and would try and sneak around in the afternoons, popping into the *rondavel* overlooking the mountains that changed every day, where Melea was usually looking after the young Tana and her cousins, pretty little things, all of them.

'How are the girls this morning? Melea, oh Melea,' he would say, trying to be as charming as possible. *'Com estei?'*

'He! Wena,' she would reply and laugh. She told the little girls to say hello: 'Say hello to Mr Fernandez, Delia, Mimi, Tana.' Which they politely did, all curtseys and ribbons like something out of a Pears soap ad, except they didn't wear many clothes apart from

bonnets and had the same ungovernable look in their eyes, like the new Mrs Tooley.

After some weeks, Fernandez and Melea begin slipping off for the odd stroll around the garden, leaving the girls to play by themselves. Their romance blossomed to the whisper of breezes in the bluegums, the flowering of happy yellow daisies, to the heady buzz of bees in the avocado orchards and the sound of the new Mrs Tooley barking out incessant instructions to her poor gardeners.

'Why are you so slow?' she shouted patronisingly at a worker who cowered in shame. She was always yelling at some worker or other to hurry up, to plant this, to dig up that. And then would turn, as if on a tickey, and wave gracefully and smilingly at Fernandez and Melea.

'The boss has a pretty wife,' said Fernandez. Melea giggled and pretended to be shocked.

Fernandez told Melea about his life in LM, and how he had come out to Africa on a ship. He told her about the white sands that line the shores of the warm ocean off Moçambique, about the fish market of LM, the bull rings, the buildings, the culture, the food. And how glad he was that he had found his way to Agatha.

'That's a lovely flower,' said Melea, pointing at the new azaleas that were starting to go all showy, like bridesmaids, flaunting and flushing and flirting, oranges next to cerise, pinks against peaches.

How is it, asked Melea, that one plant is flowering and the other one right next to it still has closed buds, waiting to open.

'Oh, they are subject to the whims of nature,' explained Fernandez carefully. 'To the mysteries of life and light, to the pollination of the bees, the temperature of the sun, the frequency of the rain ... such marvellous things.'

'They look like they're having a party,' she said.

'Oh, they do look like they're having fun,' he agreed, lightly touching her shoulder.

They strolled down to the clubhouse, which they both decided was the best view in the world, a dizzying, giddy vista across the Northern Drakensberg. It made you feel frivolous – it was so wide, with such possibility. You were an instant ruler of your own kingdom; immediate captain of a magical ship, except now Fernandez was trembling not as a result of sea legs or rum, but because of the presence of the beautiful brown thing sitting next to him.

They sat holding hands and flirting and laughing. Beneath the bench on which they were sitting, the groundcover comprised a series of variegated plants, some striped, as if they were in uniform, some speckled, some patterned like zebras. Melea's favourite was the green one with tiny pink spots, like a bird's egg, that looked like it had been spray-painted by naughty fairies in the night. They heard the sound of purple-crested loeries cackling and hooting in the trees – such an ugly noise for such a pretty bird, remarked Fernandez, as one flew by exposing its ruby red wings.

My grandmother Ess Tooley wore a real red ruby that night for the dinner party that the Tooleys were hosting for a select few from the district. Their dinner parties were lively affairs filled with discussion about war and malaria and loaded with the possibility of flirtatious exchange. Food was always secondary to social concerns, and the dinner guests constituted a powerful sector of the settler community that was growing in Agatha.

Guests began arriving before nightfall and gathered on the stoep of Kings Walden to warm up with a few cocktails and watch the night fall on the mountains. Billo Tooley's view definitely ranked amongst the best they had seen, agreed most guests, as the servants darted about with silver trays bearing the latest crystal glasses from Europe.

If you listened carefully you could hear the gasps and twitters from lady visitors who had never seen the view before.

Billo Tooley always stood head and shoulders above the rest, cutting a Great Gatsby-esque figure, although he wasn't a furtive loner at all, but a gregarious, charming, good-looking man who had the gift of making people feel instantly important and at home.

'Another G&T for a beautiful lady?' he asked Petie, his wife's sister, who was a smaller, plumper and redder version of Ess. Less beautiful, but still attractive, with fine cheekbones and a lovely tinkly laugh.

'Oh, why not,' she answered, holding her glass out and cocking her head coquettishly to one side.

'Make that two,' said her husband Popsa stepping forward. 'Take it from me tonic's still good for malaria.'

The tales of his adventures in combating malaria made him excellent value at dinner parties. Having discovered the breeding cycle of the *Anopheles* mosquito and how to break it, De Meillon had started the new malaria institute in town along with his arch rival Siegfried Annecke. It was less De Meillon's descriptions of his fieldwork than his vitriolic accounts of his colleague that were so entertaining.

'Damned fool can barely grasp the concept of head, thorax and abdomen,' said Popsa, taking a swig of his gin and tonic.

'How are things, Mr Keller?' said Billo Tooley, moving on to greet his neighbour, meaning of course one who conveniently lived some miles away. Then he shook hands with Claude Wheatley, the mayor of Tzaneen who eventually stood for a remarkable nine terms from the 1930s until the 1960s. 'Fine place you have here, Tooley,' replied Wheatley. 'Fine place indeed,' echoed Billy Maritz, who was standing next to him, a triple Scotch in hand.

Maritz was Tzaneen's first lawyer, a good-looking man with a strong nose and a strong presence. His full name was Gerhardus Jacobus Maritz and his offices were next door to Lowveld Butchery. He was one of the few Afrikaners that my grandfather befriended; he liked the man. His cases were interesting and they had satisfying arguments late into the night over hearty Scotches and cigars fat as goose droppings. Maritz later sentenced the Tzaneen Killer to hang, and went on to become Deputy Sheriff.

'Has Hymie got you with his trick yet?' said Maritz to my grandfather, with a twinkle. Hymie Gold ran the Tzaneen Store, which stocked everything from needles and taps to saddles and soap. In the Hardware Department, Hymie had glued a coin to the counter and wired a car battery under the counter so that anyone who tried to pick up the coin would be shocked.

'Butchered any clients lately?' retorted my grandfather. The banter was beginning. Maritz's office next to Lowveld Butchery provided a source of constant mockery. The butchery had started out under a *waterbessie* tree before moving into an iron shack and finally into the shop next door to Maritz. The shop had no power so the meat was hacked by hand on a big tree stump. The butcher used huge hacksaws, long knives, sharpening steels and terrifying axes – and sawdust to collect the bits of meat and fat that flew about.

From across the room, my grand-uncle Popsa caught my grandmother's eye, and he fixed her with a direct and lustful stare. She held his gaze for a second or two and then rang the bell in her hand to signal the start of dinner. This should be fun, she thought to herself as the guests were ushered in. Dusk was falling, the dining room lit with paraffin lamps, resplendent in silver and light. There was something about these scenic beginnings that added great drama to dinner at the Tooleys.

Ess seated herself to the left of her husband, facing Popsa.

'We saw a lion in the streets of Tzaneen today,' she began as the soup bowl was placed in front of her. Naturally both men gave her their immediate and total attention and she told them how she had seen a lion while strolling down Lannie Lane near the post office.

'It turned out the lion belonged to a chap called Osmers,' she laughed, 'a lion hunter who lives out of town. He uses the tame one as a decoy to lure wild ones, and every so often they have to go to the butchery to collect meat, clearing out town in the process!'

After soup, Ess's sister Lala, who was visiting again, rose up and rang a silver bell. She was pale and looked as if she had been crying, which indeed she had. 'I'd like to read something before we continue with our dinner,' she said, and dabbed her eye with a hanky. 'The most famous little mongrel in South Africa has died of biliary in Johannesburg and the broadcasters of South Africa are disconsolate.' It was an obituary in the *Cape Argus* announcing that Henry had shuffled off this mortal coil. It was written by Mr Caprera, who ended the article with the stirring words: 'Do dogs wait for us on the other side? I hope so.'

Lala burst into tears and the main course was served. 'Is she still having an affair with that man from the orchestra?' one of the diners asked, a little too loudly.

As the dinner unfolded, the moon rose and the alcohol flowed. Ess talked to Wheatley's wife about gardening and how sad her soul was since the recent death of her favourite gardener Gertrude Jekyll, an English gardener – 'or plants woman would be more accurate' – who in my grandmother's esteemed opinion had changed the way the world gardened, indeed the way it lived, with her bold new ideas on colour and planting.

Every garden scheme should have a backbone, said my grandmother with conviction, 'A central idea beautifully phrased, as Jekyll's partner Luytens would have put it.' Jekyll had brought about a revolution in the gardening world, claimed my grandmother, raising her wine glass in salute. 'Oh her range of colour, her composition, her great ability to select from the multitude of plants available . . . How I wish I could visit her garden at Munstead Wood in Surrey,' she said. 'They say that is where her talent is best expressed.'

The intensity of her passion frightened the other women diners, who were rather more restrained and inclined to stick to the realm of the kitchen. Mrs Tooley spoke of things with such ardency, with such certainty. She seemed to be enjoying herself far too much.

'Now there was a woman who understood hardy perennials,' said my grandmother, falling back in her chair and ringing the bell for the next round of plates to be gathered away. And as she sat back, a buttery shaft of lamplight fell across her cheekbones and she looked like an actress in a romantic movie.

Across the table from Ess Albert Keller, the neighbour, was regaling her sister and the other diners with a tale about the local Tzaneen Hotel. The hotel was started in 1907, a small house owned by ex-sergeant George Morgan, with a veranda all the way around it and the words 'hotel' painted on the roof. The hotel's second owner was George Morgan's wife Celia, who ran it with the man she left him for, and then it was taken over by Charlie Malan.

Everyone met here on Saturday mornings as the news of the district did the rounds and information was exchanged in colonial code-speak, refracted by mirrors and glass, scented with smoke and perfume. Along with mayors, lawyers, doctors and adventurers, my grandparents were always fond of artists. One of my grandfather's best friends was Charles Astley Maberly, who lived on a farm near Duiwelskloof and was fond of travelling the Kruger Park by bicycle.

Albert Keller owned the garage across the road from the hotel and was an intriguing if not sometimes embarrassing source of information about the goings-on behind the scenes. Right now he was explaining to the dinner guests how the hotel's electrical system worked. 'The walls in the rooms are made of double hardboard filled with wood shavings,' he said, 'and they contain the wiring that's connected to a small Bamford diesel engine in the backyard.

'Once the Bamford broke down in the middle of game reserve season, and the guests were getting all hot and grumpy and jumpy because the fans weren't working. So Malan and I, who had been at the bar all morning, strung a temporary line across the road from the garage. Now neither of us, as you know, is electrically minded, but we deliberated long and hard, and had a couple more, and then we engineered this line over the road as best we knew and I went to switch on from my side.'

He paused for dramatic effect.

'I pulled the switch and from one of the rooms across the road I heard the most terrible scream.'

He contorted his face to express pain and anguish.

'On investigation,' he sniggered, 'it was found that a Mr Hopkins who regularly called in to repair typewriters was upstairs relaxing in the bath when the 220 volts hit him.'

Ceiling fans beat the lazy air and waiters dashed back and forth with ludicrously hot pots of tea or icy cool drinks, depending on master and madam's wish. At 12 o'clock sharp everyone left to 'go home', or 'go visiting', which could mean gambling, drinking, adultery, shooting, carousing, or all of the above.

The mild Agatha breeze carried their laughter out on to the soft subtropical night.

Chapter eleven

There is no silver laughter on moonlit breezes when I take occupation of my new house: Stone Cottage, Portion 9 Langbult Farm, Agatha. After an unpleasant round of daily negotiations with the awful Austrian seller Mr Schnitzel, I finally move in on the first of June, my late grandmother Ess's birthday.

It is an uncomfortably auspicious date.

Instead of feeling that I have been granted a maternal blessing, it feels like a curse condemning me to certain madness. You are *so* going to turn out like Ess, Steven used to say, and not only am I devastated that he won't be here to herd me through it, but I am terrified that it is happening sooner and quicker than I think.

Instead of feeling a sense of sanctuary, the relief of having my own space unleashes in me an apocalyptic torrent of pain, remorse and regret. I experience a renewed and violent wave of grief for my dead brother and his son, and for Andrew. I cannot think of my ex-husband without wanting to drive a sharp knife into a breadboard, or a pillow, or something. I have an endless and insatiable capacity for alcohol and a strong desire for destruction.

Outside it is dry and dusty in the day, leaves crackle underfoot, a cold south wind snips at my heels like an ageing irritable terrier. The morning sky is yellow and smoky. At night it is cold, the distant mountains necklaced with fires. Blazes encircle town, the mountain is lit up with strings of orange beads. Infernos rage, people lose their houses, plantations are destroyed, forests go up in smoke. It is a strange backdrop to my new life in the country, not quite the peace and quiet I imagined.

The view in front of Stone Cottage is quite unlike the view from Kings Walden. While across the hills, elaborate and beautiful gardens and their features speak of love and life and death and hope over nearly a century, mine is the *bosco*, Italian for the bush, for the dark and uncontrolled wilderness. Which around the house consists primarily of an impenetrable hedge of overgrown wild shrubs, thick with thorns and unruly and aggressive invader species. Like lantana, with its evil orange-pink flower; Mauritius thorn, cruel and spiky, with thorns that never let go; and, worse, bug weed, thick, pale, hairy, smelly. If you brush past them too roughly, they leave red weals on your skin.

Beyond the *bosco*, however, if I stand on my tiptoes, I can see a purple promise of Lowveld and, at night, the twinkle of far-off lights. To the left are hills of bluegum plantations and to the right, the outer edges of Kings Walden's garden and the top of the Dead Tree, spiny fingers sticking out, like a ghostly wave. I can see bits of bougainvillea, and a few ancient cacti, parts of the vegetable garden covered in shade cloth, like I'm looking at the tradesman's entrance.

I feel like I'm being met with an angry glare of overgrowth facing me in every direction; a hostile jury of hairy, itchy plants quite unwilling to cooperate with my desire for peace and calm. I make an effort around the house to snip a branch here, pull up a weed there, but it's all too rough and tough. I scrape away a little patch of earth and plant a few lettuces and spinach, but the seedlings are plundered in a matter of hours by a band of monkeys that pull them up and toss them away without even eating them.

What if I live in this house for forty years, I think to myself despairingly, like my grandmother did in her house, all alone, with no one to temper my daily reality, unable to detect over the slow spin of the years that I am completely stark staring crazy, unable to discern truth from imagination? What if I really *do* think that I am married to a short distance sprinter, as my grandmother thought I was? Or that I had triplets that arrived in packets, for goodness sake! What if I start burning books? Going to the Coach House and firing the workers – as she did?

And I am still trapped in a long dark peristaltic hole of self-pity and depression that has gripped me on and off for the past three years. I'm haunted by grief, terrified by violence. I haven't coped at all, I think to myself, downing endless glasses of wine; I haven't coped at all. I've simply run and self-medicated, travelled wherever I could, fled with my traumas across the world, only to wake up in Mumbai or New Orleans, Dar es Salaam or Cardiff, with the same hollow heart and the same black soul.

I tear about my new place unpacking boxes, slugging down bottles of cheap red wine and bursting into tears and fits of rage, like a child. I sob on the kitchen steps, stand at the sink and cry into the dishes like a tranquillised housewife in a sad ballad. I weep with my head on the office desk, much to the dismay of my cats who bring me presents of gnawed rat heads, entrails and giblets, smearing their bloody signature across my notebooks and magazines.

And as if to underline my crisis, the cellphone reception is a complete mystery in and around Stone Cottage. If I stand in the middle of the lounge there is a flat spot, no reception, nada, nothing. If I take two steps towards the fireplace, I hook up to the Nkowankowa towers, and get a faint signal. If I take two steps to the left, I hook up to Giyani, which is unreliable to say the least. If I take two steps forward, towards that window, I connect to the Letsitele, which flickers on and off like a Christmas tree. And in the kitchen I can jump from Tzaneen tower to Gravelotte in a matter of steps. Ninety per cent of my conversations seem to go: 'You're breaking up, you sound like you're at the bottom of the pool; shall I call you back? Where on earth are you?'

And the water that comes out of the house taps is a disturbingly sludgy brown. I conduct a test: I pour tap water into a big glass and let in stand in sunlight for an hour or two. It looks like a bad biology experiment and I'm sure I can see pond scum floating, fur-like, at the bottom. It takes about three hours to run the bath, and I can't see my own body when I'm in it, which is not such a bad thing considering how fat I've become. There is a trickle of water in the river below the house, but it's practically impossible to get there since my walking shoes walked off with the armed robbers and I'm hobbling about in a pair of smelly and decaying old takkies.

Sensing my despair, my mother takes practical steps to extend a line of civilisation across the valley. 'I'm sending a runner,' she says on the phone. And so begins the courier system between our two houses. The runner is either Elias or Franz, both garden workers, who are dispatched frequently with bottles of wine, cat food, smoked trout, cigarettes, newspapers and sometimes even handwritten invitations to dinner.

My mind feels like a cage of anxious prowling panthers. My sleep is broken, jagged and wracked with nightmares: bloody beds, severed heads, men with guns. One night I dream that I am being chased by a paedophile priest who has already killed one person with a big sword. He runs a racket under the auspices of selling glassware and religious knick-knacks and I am in his shop admiring the kitsch when I realise I am in mortal danger. Sometimes I wake up with such a shock that I leap demonically out of bed.

I dream endlessly about buildings and travel. In every dream I'm leaving or arriving. There are boats and aeroplanes, buses and ships, trains, scooters, cars, funiculars, escalators, steps, every conceivable form of transport. I find myself in tall swaying buildings in a part of town that keeps recurring and yet doesn't exist in reality. There are sky-walks. I have to make impossible leaps through spaces that are wildly architectural and hyper-real. Every day I wake up exhausted. I feel like I have been alive for hundreds of years, a tormented soul that can't escape this groundhog day of tragedy – every phone call another death, every funeral another desperate occasion, every attempt at recovery met by another blow.

And then a technical problem strikes one of the power lines in Agatha and the district is plunged into darkness over a long weekend. I have firewood and candles, but need kindling and set out with a panga and a bottle of beer to gather sticks to start a fire since Stone Cottage is rapidly dropping to the temperature of a walk-in fridge. I put on my beanie and tracksuit and head with some trepidation to the edges of the *bosco,* breaking off bits of branches, collecting sticks into a basket, pulling at the odd branch or two.

After the first load I sit panting on the stoep and notice, with great irritation, an old stone and concrete braai next to the house. Ugly damn thing, I think, and then remember I have a ten pound hammer somewhere in one of the ex's boxes. I drop the firewood, head for the hammer and set about destroying the braai.

The sun is setting by the time I have finished screaming and shouting and hammering down the braai monstrosity. I am sweating like a pig and feel much better. I have swung and smashed – fuck fuck you fuck you with every swing – until my arms ache and I can barely walk. I start the fire by pouring a cup of paraffin on to a couple of logs, light some candles and attack a bottle of red wine.

I spend the night at the fire all alone in my old dark stone cottage, saddened to the point of madness, and enraged with it, cursing everyone who has ever wronged me – and God knows it appears the list is endless: my ex-husband, my ex-boyfriends, the armed robbers, the bad friends, the school headmaster, the bank manager, my ex-boss … I fling things across the room and stamp my feet in rage. I wail and cry into the night, dropping glasses and staggering like a fool.

The worst thing about trauma is the clutter. Nothing is calm, nothing is quiet. My mind is filled with brutish thoughts, dark images, fears and jagged lights glancing off knives. I keep seeing my brother's dead feet, Benjamin's dead face, cold and blue, like a baby gargoyle, in a grey hospital blanket on a cold metal table; blood on the floor in Andrew's studio, the extraordinary feeling of a gun against my temple. I can see the pinpoints of rage in my ex-husband's blue eyes when he left me once and said, quoting a David Grey song: 'I just wanna a nice little housewife who'll give me a steady life and not keep going off the rails'.

I'll show you rails, you bastard, I think furiously.

What can I really say about the volatility of the past few years? I never intended it. I fell in love, got married, set off for the city to take up a fabulous new job … Then my brother died, I moved house, my husband went to live in Cape Town for six months, my nephew died, I bought a house, my friend Andrew was murdered, I left my job, had an armed robbery … and then the terrible realisation that in order to heal I had to leave the man I no longer loved and had in fact ceased loving some time ago.

What the fuck was I supposed to do? Stay sane?

I wake up on the couch with a blanket over me and all the cats. The first thing I see is the dying end of a fire and a scattering of bottles and glasses, books and ornaments. The cow skin rug has developed great big red wine stains and looks like it was caught in a shoot-out. I stagger to my feet, putting one of them in an ashtray full of butts which overturns and scatters over the cow skin.

'Fuuuuccccccccccck!' I scream.

I stagger to the kitchen door, fling it open and scream a string of hideous curses at the daylight. Fortunately I have a gas stove, so tea is possible, but the fridge is starting to melt, and the tiled floor is cold and unwelcoming. I pour a fat Scotch with sludgy tap water, down it, and then throw my cellphone at the wall.

God knows, we seek consolation in alcohol and drugs – they satisfy our longing to return to a childlike state of innocence, to be unaware of consequence. And God knows I have explored those horizons. I kick-start the fire and sit for another eternity of a morning, torturing myself with pitiful thoughts of what a disappointment I've been. To myself, to my family, to the world.

'I didn't have a chance,' I weep aloud. 'I was fucked from the start.' From the time I became an adult my overwhelming feeling was that everything around me was completely crazy. Wrong place, wrong time, I was coughed up on the pebbled shores of a world inhabited by strange creatures with odd ideas.

I spend the next two days hunting and gathering firewood, drinking anything I can lay my hands on, uttering curses to the gods who took my brother and friends, bemoaning my own spiritual bankruptcy, my own madness and wildness, and mourning what feels like the absolute loss of innocence. Death, murder, madness, financial ruin … it has been a war of attrition on my hope and faith in humanity. I have been stripped to a crazed core.

'I knew it was going to be a disaster,' I weep, thinking of my first sense of a loss of innocence as a pre-teen child, the dawning and excruciating realisation that my worst fears were being confirmed: the adult world was indeed populated by drunkards, womanisers, liars, cheats, philanderers, actresses and thieves, all parading under the guise of normal suburbanite professionals and parents.

I found adults to be smelly things with evil intentions and crocodile smiles. I felt like an alien child that had landed in the middle of a bizarre play. My teachers were authoritarian, bad-tempered, old-fashioned. The local Brownies refused to enrol me, I was asked to leave ballet classes, and grudgingly gave up wearing boys' clothes as my breasts started budding and men began peering lasciviously. Boys around me started blushing and squeaking and sweating as their voices dropped and their bodies grew, in spurts and jerks, like the hands of a railway station clock. And then there were the appalling discoveries of sex and bodies: 'What's rape?' I asked Steven one night in a whisper. 'Force fuck,' he whispered back.

As I figured out the first stirrings of human motive and consequence, it seemed that despite its veneer of normalcy, white seventies suburbia was not just an odd place – it was, in fact, stark staring crazy. Home was volatile. My father went away often, high-balling his way through the PR scene and its pretty girls, and when he was gone my mother gathered us about and threw teapots and cups at the wall. Brett tried to reason with her. Steven cried. I watched.

Brett had a girlfriend and was discovering sex. Tana instructed us to whistle and knock before we went to his room. Steven was dangerously hooligan. He had teamed up with the neighbour's son and they spent their time bunking school, shooting birds, their friends, their sisters and the elderly with pellet guns, concocting explosives and experimenting with new and interesting ways to tap into the neighbourhood power grid and telephone line network.

The lounge was often full of weeping women just like my mother, drinking wine and smoking cigarettes before lunch. They were mostly pretty, fashionable and having affairs. The mother of one of my best friends became an alcoholic and in the mornings we fetched her and her sister from their flat down the road. I waited in the car and Tana went to collect the girls whose mother lay in a stupor, empty gin bottles floating in the cistern, tucked away in the cupboards, rolling out from under the beds.

Outside, on the streets, there was tension, *baasskap*, weirdness in the air. There were corridor rumours about the violent natives that were coming to get us, talk of barbarians and apocalypse. People were horrible to their servants, many beat them. Outside our house however, came the smell of sin and the sounds of laughter from Melea's room.

Although the house and the interiors became unkempt and poorly maintained as my grandmother aged, Kings Walden remained my uber-sanctuary. The garden took priority over the house and the dogs, cats, chickens, wild cats, rats, mice and lizards all moved in and filled the spaces where people once lived. In some places the walls were crumbling and the floor boards sagging. And the roof was looking patchy.

I loved it.

Lala, my great-aunt, had moved into one of the guest rooms and was in the throes of dying. She was mad, dribbling and incontinent, a far cry from when she lit up the airwaves with her lilting voice and the cheery bark of Henry the terrier. I walked with her and Melea in the day. Melea shuffled her along as I pointed out the flowers and plants and insects to my drugged, crazed great-aunt who was 'deteriorating', according to what I could glean from adult conversation.

Because I only partially grasped the concept of consequence, never mind mental illness, it wasn't frightening to me at all. And Melea could do a fantastic Shakespearean rendition of Lala – staggering and drooling like a drunk, with her eyes rolling and her tongue hanging out – which had me in stitches, especially so because she did it behind Lala's back.

Other times we were taken over to Lovely Cottage, where my grand-uncle Popsa had returned to continue his mosquito studies and his war against malaria. When it was Feeding Time, he would shout out at us and we would tiptoe quietly into his 'mosquito room', a dark creeper-walled study filled with piles of books, microscopes, boxes, glasses and tanks of live mosquitoes, regarded by us with a compelling mixture of fear and fascination.

Steven and I would slide our forearms into the tanks where the mosquitoes lived. Screened off by a plate of glass and illuminated by a bright fluorescent light, they didn't seem like our own arms at all. They were enlarged and hyper-real. And then we would all watch as a small flock of female mosquitoes landed on one or both of our pale pink forearms.

'Come along, bite you little buggers!' yelled Popsa.

Which eventually they did. It was a fat red sting followed by a horrible burning sensation.

My grand-uncle would take a sample of blood, rub the sting with disinfectant and shoo us back outside again. 'Put on some bulbinella,' he would shout, referring to the bulbous plant that grows wild here and is good for bites, stings, rashes and allergies. Steven didn't seem to mind Feeding Time, he didn't even mind going on monkey shooting expeditions with Popsa, but I found it awful and I found him bad-mannered and too fondly-fondly. Perhaps if I had known then that I was playing such a significant role in combating the scourge of malaria I may have acted with better grace.

The only person who seemed normal was my grandmother. 'Don't worry about them, they're all mad, dear,' was what she said comfortingly when I complained of the reign of terror to which I felt I was subject, be it Feeding Time, driving lesson time with my brothers – 'Bridgie must get on top of the roof rack otherwise I'm not driving' – my parents fighting and smashing wine glasses, or the strange voodoo goings-on in the compound.

I still slept with her at night when we were at Kings Walden. She made us very sweet tea with condensed milk and then everyone from the cats and dogs to the week-old chicks would get into her

Three generations: Ess, Tana and Bridget

big, soft, saggy, sandy bed and the rest of the world would cease to matter.

She was my heroine, capable of running the world. She ran her own with such zeal and clarity. Her garden was her *paramour*, as she called it, and one of my favourite things was to be shown around the 'new developments' which could include anything from the flowering of a granadilla hedge or the installation of a water feature to the razing to the ground of an unwitting rondavel.

I thought her scope of thinking and doing tremendously wide. I remember her decision to remove a tree-lined avenue of bluegums. She commandeered the operation with military precision. We left home at ungodly hours in her blue Ranchero to 'meet the fellers' – said with a merry twinkle – to supervise the removal of the logs, meet the dynamite man, check up on the operation and 'tell those lazy bastards to get a move on'. When it came to blowing up the avenue of stumps, Steven was allowed to push the detonator and we watched the force travel along the cable and the tree stump explode into the air with a great big bang of dust and wood and smoke like a civil war.

'Now, my darlings,' said my grandmother to us three children one morning, 'you are to take this vase of beautiful blue agapanthus and put it next to Lala's bed. As you know, she is very ill and the doctor is coming here soon to help her go to sleep. It is time for you to say goodbye.'

'Is she going to sleep for ever?' asked Steven.

'Yes,' said my grandmother. 'It is her time to go to sleep.'

'She will sleep nicely in the ground,' said Melea, who was doing all the finishing touches in Lala's room, like fresh linen and cotton blankets, making sure the windows were clean and the floor swept. Earlier on she had washed Lala, dressed her in a beautiful lacy nightie and dabbed on some face powder and lipstick.

'Goodbye Lala, have a nice time and we love you,' I said to my great-aunt who lay looking pale and beautiful and non compos mentis in her bedroom.

'I hope you like the blue agatha panthers that we put in the vase there,' said Steven.

'You were a fantastic aunt,' said Brett, ever the oldest and most diplomatic, 'and thank you for all the times you played the piano for us and for all the joy that Henry brought the world.'

Her bedroom was awash with sunlight and the smell of soap and perfume and flowers. It was so peaceful. Next to her bed was a big photograph of Henry and a smaller one of her husband Tom. There was a framed newspaper cutting with a picture of her and Mr Caprera from the orchestra, and Henry. There was a beautiful spray of sweet peas that scented the dressing table and, next to it, our big vase of blue agapanthus.

Then old Dr Boon arrived and there was a flurry of bell ringing, tea making and shooing out of dogs and children. We went outside for a while and played in the garden and then eventually my mother and my grandmother and Melea came into the kitchen looking relieved and Melea poured them all snifters of cognac, and an especially strong one for Dr Boon, who was looking most solemn.

No wonder I ended up weird, I say to myself, slumped alone on the couch in my old Stone Cottage.

Shrubs grow wild, unpruned trees take on strange forms, branches fall, beds disappear and creepers become ever entangled. The day turns to night and the night turns to daybreak. It is nearly dawn and I am full of maudlin and vodka. I shuffle to the stoep – the morning sky is like an orange mackerel – and I decide, on a whim and a stagger, to take a walk up to the family cemetery, which is a good few kilometres away. I am drunk. I teeter out the house wearing tracksuit, beanie and a daypack into which the bottle of

Tana and Brett, Durban

vodka is jammed, wrapped in a sarong.

It is a kilometre or so uphill to the top of the road, and then a flat walk along a mud road with a pale *middelmannetjie* bleached blonde by the winter sun and dryness. The birds are twittering and chattering. I am feeling hopeless and old. I think of those empty mornings driving home from the *jol*, watching the joggers jog smugly and vigorously past, puffing and panting as my own breath stinks of cigarettes and alcohol and cocaine.

A wrought iron gate leads into the cemetery, which overlooks the mountains that change every day. Set beneath a grove of bluegums that whisper endlessly into the winds, the cemetery consists of a series of graves of my ancestors and more immediate family. The main feature is a giant *waterbessie* tree, underneath which there is a concrete bench and a table with a concrete book upon it, inscribed with the words: Darling Ess and Tana, Billo's Garden of Remembrance 1954.

The cold morning air has made me feel temporarily better. I walk up to my brother and Benjamin's headstone. 'Morning, boys,' I say cheerily. I lean against the headstone, take the vodka from the backpack and have a hearty swig. 'Aaaarrhgh,' I gurgle as the fiery white liquid burns a hole down my oesophagus, then 'Morning boys' again, louder. Underneath the trees, near my grandmother's grave, I catch sight of a very old monkey wandering painfully and arthritically through the wintry undergrowth.

I burst into tears.

And then through the vodka and snot-soaked river of tears pouring down my face, I notice a small figure approaching. It is an old woman, backlit by the rising orange sun, so all I can see is her silhouette. When she comes closer and stands at the cemetery gate I realise it is old Mama Gidjane.

She takes my hand, her old eyes are misted over, a glassy cataract blue. She is barefoot, a brightly coloured pink and orange traditional cloth draped over her shoulders, a string of coloured beads around her neck and a simple red woollen bracelet indicating her status as a *sangoma* or traditional healer.

Mama Gidjane has been a peripheral yet significant presence throughout my life. When we were children we would go with her and watch her 'throw the bones' at the compound – an activity to which I attribute Steven's lifelong fascination with things ritual and voodoo. People's lives changed according to her predictions and pronouncements, and she had a very wise look in her eyes, as if she had been alive for ever. She was Melea's backup and adviser and appeared, like a pop-up figure, at all the important events in our family life.

Once my parents were returning from a Sunday afternoon walk when they came across a group of farm workers gathered round the pathetically beaten and bleeding body of a fellow worker.

'He is a wizard!' shouted the crowd. 'He flew in on the storm and knocked over a pine tree.'

Next to the accused man lay the fallen pine tree.

He must die, they said. He has knocked over the tree and he is causing sickness and death.

The bleeding wizard groaned.

My father gazed at the crowd, uncertain as to how his liberal instinct should rule on this one. And then he remembered Mama Gidjane and she was summoned to sort out the situation. Eventually the wizard was released, the crowd reluctantly dispersed and the fallen pine tree was turned into bookshelves for my father's library.

'Le kae mabula,' says Mama Gidjane, when she comes closer. *Eish wena*, she takes my hand.

'Mama Gidjane,' I reply. *'Go bjang?'* (How are you?)

'Ke lokile, wena?' (Fine and you?)

'Go bjang?' she asks again. (How are you?)

'Ga go loke selo,' I say, shaking my head. (Oh, it's been bad.) *'Ke kwa bohloko kudu.'* (Lots of pain, too much pain ...)

'Cha cha e ntshi kudu,' she says, shaking her head. (Too much cha cha.) She waves her hand over her mouth to indicate that I stink of alcohol, and then starts laughing ...

'Ke nyaka segalagala, mammie?' I say to her. (Do you want some hot stuff?)

She takes the bottle, pours herself a capful and downs it. She does this three times and then gives it back to me.

'Now you,' she says.

I take a slug straight from the bottle.

'Jona, joo,' she says, and then tells me to sit down on the bench. She sits next to me, burps, laughs, and then undoes her little bag – it looks like it's made out of a rabbit skin or that of a mongoose perhaps. From it she produces a cloth filled with shells and bones and strange bits of things – mirrors, teeth, tiny bones and scraps of fur.

Life is a difficult thing, she says in her broken English. She gestures to her heart and to her head. People came here many, many years ago. There has been suffering since the beginning of time. People have lost their loved ones through wars and floods and drought, they have lost their loved ones through accidents and tragedies and crime and bad luck, they have lost their homes, their hearts, their happiness. I am not the only one with pain, she says, shaking her head.

She spreads the cloth on the bench and in the centre places a beautiful round stone. *'Wena'* (You), she points at me and holds my gaze. *'Wena o wena'* (That is you), she says, indicating towards the stone. All around the stone she puts her little trinkets, and each time she puts one down, she points to a different part of my body and tells me that this is me. My heart is a lynx's tooth, my body is a silver marble, my head a cane rat femur, my stomach a chip of gemsbok horn, my laughter a piece of pink plastic mirror ...

To heal myself, she tells me, I have to sit down with all my pieces. I must be aware of every part of myself, be aware of my own losses, demons, madness and quirks. It's like healing a country, I have to 'make like Codesa', she says, laughing, referring to the negotiating team that brokered a democratic settlement in 1994. She takes the bottle of vodka and has a hearty slug.

I must put myself and all my pieces around a negotiation table, she says, warming to her own metaphor.

I picture myself sitting round a table with Bridget in a variety of horrifying guises. The griever, the mourner; the wild girl, the private person, the careerist; the struggler, the drinker and druggie; the lover, the artist ...

I take another slug of vodka.

It is a slow process, says Mama Gidjane, but I have to accept that I have all these pieces and I have to live with them.

She scratches around in her cloth and takes out a little plastic bottle of herbs. She takes a pinch out and places it in a small green plastic cup that she unearths from under her sarong. She adds a generous dash of vodka.

'Drink,' she says.

I down the mixture which is a horribly bitter concoction.

'And you?' I say, unsteadily.

'*Aowa,*' she says, shaking her head. 'Only for you.'

Her voice is slow and gravelly, she holds my hand tightly. I can smell tobacco and woodsmoke on her clothes, a tinge of Zambuk, a whiff of muti. The sun is rising higher in the sky now and my head feels floaty.

'*Badimo ba re o dire tshengwana,*' she tells me. (Your ancestors say you must make a garden.) They are all there, but they are gone, they are living in another room, another world. It is not below the ground, she says, it is not in the sky. It is just another room that we can't see, except in our dreams and our memories, except in our love of the earth and of life. If you want to open the door you must make a garden, she says, make a garden like your *gugu*, like your mama.

'You must be strong,' she says, taking the bottle of vodka away from me. 'Make a garden. *Tsamaya,*' she says, shaking her hand at me. Go. She waves at me as if I have been dismissed, and turns to leave the cemetery.

She stops at the gate. '*Gopola kgwele ya mmollo!*' she shouts out. (Remember the ball of fire!) And then, vodka bottle in hand, she walks out the gate and starts picking her way down the road again, towards the ever rising sun.

Chapter twelve

My grandmother drained a glass of Scotch, dropped to her knees on the lawn overlooking the mountains that change every day, and wept furiously. She threw the glass into the darkening edges of the garden, held her head in her hands and felt the hot tears fall through her fingers on to the cool grass.

Her husband Billo had been diagnosed with cancer. 'Elsie, my darling,' he had said the evening before. They were sitting on the stoep having a pre-dinner drink. 'Elsie, my darling, I need to tell you something.'

She looked at him in the fading pink light and her heart filled with fondness and warmth. 'Dr Boon tells me I have stomach cancer.'

'What?'

'I went to see him, I haven't been feeling well, I've been having pain and ... he did some tests ... I have cancer.'

'What are we going to do?' cried Ess, holding on to her husband's shoulders as the night fell and the bottom dropped out of her world.

The doctor prescribed a change of diet and morphine for the pain. He showed Billo how to administer the morphine. 'First you tie a tourniquet, make a fist, pump your arm so that the vein bulges right out, like that.' The vein on Billo's arm stood out like an angry blue snake. 'Fill this syringe' – it was a large silver one – 'make sure there are no air bubbles ... then you inject directly into the vein, slowly, keeping as steady as possible, until the syringe is empty. Pull it out slowly, relax your arm ... It works very quickly.'

He also showed Ess how to inject the morphine, where to keep it – somewhere cool and dry and out of reach of animals and servants – and how to keep everything clean and hygienic. He was hesitant to have this discussion with Mrs Tooley's young daughter present, but she insisted.

'If her father is ill, she should know about it,' said Mrs Tooley, and so Tana also learned how to inject her father, how to find his vein, how much morphine to use, and what to expect of course, once it had been done. 'Not really the time to discuss the weather,' as Dr Boon politely put it. And then, philosophically, added, 'On the other hand, it's probably an excellent time to talk about the weather.'

'Your father is ill,' my grandmother said to Tana, 'and he's going to die eventually. The worst part of his illness is the pain. If he is in pain you are to help him with his medicine. Do not be afraid of it. Do not be afraid of him dying either, it will be a relief in the end, probably to all of us, but mostly to him.'

Billo decided Tana should be sent, with Mimi and Delia, her cousins, to boarding school at Parktown Convent in Johannesburg. 'It will be better for her not to see me ill,' said Billo, as his wife wept at the thought of her lovely wild daughter having to put on a uniform – and shoes – and be confined to a dormitory, be looked after by nuns, horrible nuns, be made to sit in a hot classroom and learn Latin and algebra and stupid things like that.

'She'll hate the place,' protested Ess. 'She'll hate the nuns, her spirit will be strangled.'

'I don't want my daughter to see me deteriorate. It will be worse for her to see that and, Elsie, my dear, a good education is most important for young women these days. I shall tell her of our decision at dinner tonight.'

My grandmother rose to her feet and walked off into the garden. Clouds were gathering, great big fat white clouds that were bringing rain. There was a smell of moisture in the air, a saltiness, a viscosity. The clouds were coming from the east, rain was imminent, a storm certain.

Billo sat in his bedroom overlooking the mountains and watched his beautiful wife disappear into the foliage. He felt sore, tired, desolate. How pain weakens a man, he thought, holding his stomach which responded with an uneasy twinge and a rush of nausea. He watched the skies darken outside, the clouds pick up speed and volume. He saw lightning bounce off the mountains, heard the first big fat raindrops start to tap-tap on the farmhouse roof.

My mother Tana was in the bath, as yet blissfully unaware of her future. She stretched out – her coltish legs seemed to get longer by the day – and smiled at the two cats that were perched plumply on the side of the bath watching her. She heard the sound of rain start to hammer on the roof and pulled herself lazily up to a sitting position. There was a nearby rumble of thunder, a click of electricity in the air and the two cats leapt off the bath edge and fled.

From the bottom of the garden my grandmother Ess saw the lightning bouncing around the mountains, getting closer and closer with each strike. The rain was getting heavier, her hair was damp, her blouse wet. She stood at the bottom of the stairs, near the clubhouse and looked up at the silhouette of Kings Walden farmhouse, her shattered castle, her broken dream. From behind the curtains came the deceptively comforting twinkle of lights. And she watched in disbelief as a great big bolt of lightning came out of the skies and hit the side of the house with a loud crash. She let out a high-pitched scream and started running.

'I'm fine, I'm fine,' gasped Tana who had been flung clean out of the bath when the lightning hit the side of the house. She was lying on the floor, her hair static, eyes wild. 'Really, I'm all right.'

'Stand up, let me look at you,' said Ess. 'Are you sure nothing is burnt or hurt?'

But my mother was fine, unsteady at first, but miraculously unscathed.

'Your father wants to send you to boarding school, my darling,' cried Ess, suddenly clutching her damp and startled daughter. 'He doesn't want you to see him ill ... he has cancer ...' and she started crying.

'I'm going to make a garden for him,' replied my mother. She put on her dressing gown and went to her bedroom.

There were three matriarchs on the platform of the Tzaneen station to say goodbye to Tana, Delia and Mimi, who were all uniformed and weeping and being sent off to Parktown Convent with Petie. Billo Tooley bade a formal goodbye to his beautiful young daughter from his study in the farmhouse. Do your best, he said to her, and she did not see the pain in his heart and the agony and the tears and the heartbreak. She did not see him weeping and clutching his dying stomach as she went off to school, all girdled and trussed.

My grandmother, Melea and Mama Gidjane saw their pinched little faces, framed in a train window, as the train pulled out of the station. My grandmother was stoic, but when the train was out of sight she sat down on the station bench and wept.

'*Jo, jo, jo,*' said Melea to Mama Gidjane. 'It is not easy being a mother.'

'*Watseba wena*' (You know), replied Mama Gidjane, life is not easy.

They stood on the platform and let Mrs Tooley weep until the sun began to get too hot in the sky and then they each took a hold of one of her hands and helped her into the coolth of the station and the first wobbly steps of her new daughter-less life.

'*Swarella matsogo a gago kgauswi le lefase*' (Keep your hands close to the earth), said Mama Gidjane and gave her a round stone with a flat bottom that fitted perfectly into her hand.

'She says you mustn't be sad, translated Melea. 'Stop feeling sorry and let's go back to your beautiful garden.'

'Gardens have always grown in response to events around them,' she said later to her sister Petie who was concerned about how much time Ess was spending on her own, how thin she was getting, how preoccupied and remote.

'I need to garden,' she said. 'It connects me to another world, it soothes my soul.'

'Gardens have always been sanctuaries, my darling,' said Petie sympathetically. 'Their first purpose was a healing one, you know. They were medicinal.'

She and Popsa had recently returned from a trip to Italy, and she had visited some of the country's famous gardens, including the world's oldest botanical garden attached to the University of Padua. Tucked into a shady corner off a side street, bordered by a lush green canal, the first living collection of plants was started here early in the sixteenth century – a botany or *semplici* department, to instruct doctors on herbal healing properties.[4]

'The early Christian hermits often settled in the ruins of Roman country villas,' continued Petie. 'And they preserved vital knowledge about gardening and plants during the Dark Ages. Returning Crusaders and travellers often brought plants to the monasteries that offered them shelter ...'

'Only good thing the bloody Christians have done,' muttered my grandmother. Despite the religiosity of her own Edwardian education, she had never been a believer. Her husband's illness, her daughter's unhappy departure to a Catholic boarding school, had provoked in her a deep crisis, the solution to which was not faith but intense gardening. She sighed loudly.

'It was the Christians who developed the idea of the Garden of Eden as a model for their actual gardens, you know,' said Petie. 'They thought of them as the ideal world, perfection in the wilderness. In medieval times it was the *hortus conclusus* – the enclosed garden – symbolising the womb of the Virgin Mary.'

Ess rolled her eyes heavenwards.

'Now the garden became the opposite of the *selva* – the wild forest, the soul separated from the untamed world – cultivated by the grace of God within protected walls ...'

But Elsie Tooley didn't want her soul separated from the untamed world. She wanted her *selva*, her soul, to be part of the wild forest, to be fed by its springs, shaded by its trees, enchanted by its flowers. Religious notions of the Garden of Eden had no place in Agatha or her garden as far as she was concerned.

'I'd like to see a pale Italian Catholic priest repel some of those

---

[4] Judith Chatfield, *The Classic Italian Garden.*

tough and ghastly creeping underground stems we get here in late spring,' she replied. 'Not even God can stop Nature's fifth column, you know.'

'Oh Ess,' sighed Petie, 'you are such a tough customer.'

My mother hated being away from home and hated the nuns of Parktown Convent even more. They wore hair shirts, she cried, and smelt terrible. They didn't wash and their minds were poisoned and treacherous. They were evil. The postcards were unhappy, the holidays emotional. And for everyone Billo's cancer was a difficult thing with which to cope.

Ess's gardening offered a soulful antidote to the crises in her life, life with its riddles and mysteries and questions, life with its pain and unpredictability. She ordered as many gardening books as she could, from Johannesburg, from London, from America and Canada – books on shrubs and groundcovers, books on wildflowers, books on pergolas, water gardens, Japanese gardens and formal English gardens. She began a lifelong habit of filching plants and cuttings from other people's gardens, and began taking a more vigorous interest in planning and designing, declaring her garden a ship that would sail into the gentle seas symbolised by the Lowveld beyond.

In the evenings on the stoep, when they met for their drink in front of the mountains that change every day, Ess Tooley and her husband talked about life and love and how sad it was that he was going to die. To take his mind off things and stroke his soul, she read to him excerpts from her new gardening books.

'Gardens first flourished in Tuscany,' she read one evening, 'cradle of the humanist movement. They played a significant role in the teachings of the early Church fathers, and ancient Roman texts inspired a love for country villa life. In Tuscany the designs were mainly defined by evergreen material, in Rome by architectural use of stone. Water flowed through fountains and nymphaeums (grottoes dedicated to the nymphs) which was most important in the hot Italian climate ...'

She described to him the ideal garden, a geometric evergreen garden, as conceived in the mid 1500s – one that included pergolas, lawns, clipped hedges, topiary – preferably spelling out the owner's name – grottoes and a summer house. The grandest sported geometrical parterres, labyrinths, fountains and grottoes and, beyond that, orchards and game preserves, 'the ever-vaster garden dissolved in the distance into the *bosco* – a shady grove of trees implying a wilderness'.[5]

Billo loved the descriptions of the early Italian monastery gardens. They had an outlying *orto* for vegetables, fruit trees and a grape arbour. Sometimes a burial ground was combined with an orchard and was a place for monks to walk, conversing with each other or in solitary contemplation. Often a church had a west entrance with a courtyard, designated a Paradise with flower beds and fruit trees. This was a spot of sanctuary for those fleeing secular persecution.

'Oh, make me a sanctuary in which I can flee my persecution,' implored my grandfather Billo. 'Make me a garden where I can escape, where I can be free of pain.'

'I will make you a garden *segreto*, my darling,' cried Ess, 'a special place that shall be your sanctuary and your escape. It will be cool and shady, with delicious monsters and lilies, with elephant ears and jungly creepers. I'll plant candytuft and cineraria, I'll plant hollyhocks and larkspur, Virginia stocks and ...'

'Just don't put any religious things in it,' said Billo, 'and no wandering monks.'

My grandmother gave him a faux withering look.

---

[5] Judith Chatfield, *The Classic Italian Garden*.

But each time he talked of his pain it pained her too, so terribly. And every time she thought of his and her pains, she planted another flower, another shrub, herb or creeper. She planted dusty millers, Paris daisies, flame peas and blue butterfly bushes. She planted Japanese lanterns, fuchsias and azaleas, rhododendron, ranunculus and salvia.

Every time my mother came home she was amazed and enchanted to see how much the Kings Walden garden had grown and changed and flourished. She took over Billo's garden from her mother and added her own touches to it – another concrete fountain, a bold tree fern, a bank of basil, the odd red rose. Every time she came home, however, she was devastated to see how her father was deteriorating. It was as if his garden grew in direct proportion to his suffering.

Sometimes he walked with Tana and her cousins Mimi and Delia up to the shed at the top of the house where he kept cows, and other times – if he was feeling strong – he would take them round the farm and show them the packing shed, the dams, the litchi and avo orchards, the 'obnoxious weeds' that needed spraying. Ess took photographs: Tennis Tea House, 1948; Billo and Ess drinking tea at Cat's Lawn, 1949; Picnic at Heronmere, 1950; Billo and Delia at Rocky Falls, 1952.

But his pain eventually became too volatile for him to walk or drive, and sometimes he would beg his daughter to take him to his garden, and they would sit in the shade of a giant *mnali* tree, where the arum lilies grew, granadillas flowered like a garden of Paradise and the scent of the little pennyroyal lawn covered the smell of pain and morphine. 'Oh, please do it now,' groaned my grandfather, and my mother would lie him down on the blanket on the grass, and inject him slowly and carefully with the silver syringe.

As the morphine took hold, my grandfather exhaled, and let himself be soothed by the sound of cooing birds, the warmth of the blanket and the moistness of the cool grotto. He saw the faces of concrete lions melting into rivers, he heard the trilling of insects amplify and recede. His daughter, like his wife, read to him from gardening books and he felt his pain begin to recede, like the tide washing out to sea.

There was a time, read my mother from Wordsworth,
when meadow, grove and stream,
The earth, and every common sight,
To me did seem
Apparelled in celestial light,
The glory and the freshness of a dream.

Billo lay floating, while my mother Tana sat on a blanket on the lawn next to him. She was reading now from a book called *Beautiful Gardens of the World.* 'Pleasure gardens are outdoor places designed by man which induce in the beholder a sense of wellbeing. Like drugs, they can be addictive ...'[6]

Her father laughed eerily.

'But unlike drugs,' she continued, 'they have no unpleasant after effects. He who sets out to write about pleasure gardens must look into himself for the answer, and if he is shrouded in the smog of Western industrial society, he will need to peer hard into the dimness for inspiration. He must examine the springs of his being and the nature of the universe and rid himself of that notion of the past, if he still has it, that the history of his species is a matter wholly of the random play of economic forces ...'

In the distance Billo saw Mama Gidjane sweeping and her actions seemed mechanical, like a clockwork sweeper. The noise of the broom – fashioned from a magic guarri tree – was rhythmic and it calmed him and the African-ness of it touched him, he felt vague visual memories of his English childhood, patchwork pictures so very different to that of Mama Gidjane with her bare feet and

---

[6] *Beautiful Gardens of the World*

144

medieval broom and behind it all, of course, the power and beauty of the mountains that change every day.

My mother carried on reading: 'The philosopher and aesthete will ask "What is beauty?", and construct their own models for an answer, but a sense that universal beauty exists has always informed the actions and beliefs of men. A study of pleasure gardens is a study of one way that man has tried to bring some part of that beauty closer to him.'

My grandfather Billo was now in full flight. Pulsing images throbbed and thrummed: the war, travelling to South Africa, Agatha, his first wife Muriel . . . soft and stretchy pictures of faces, voices, moments. He breathed in the colours of the azaleas in the distance, with their soft pinks with pale edges, he inhaled the incredible purple petals of the petrea bush, imagined himself as chlorophyll in a monkey flower. He felt his pain disappear and the beauty of the garden in all its glory filled his heart with love and relief.

Chapter thirteen

The winter starts rolling past. It is still cold enough though, at night, to make a fire, and tonight I am sitting at the fireside in my parents' guest house, in the very same bedroom in which my grandmother Ess and I saw the fireball. My parents have gone away again, leaving me in charge. I am happy to be away from my brooding old stone cottage and its foreboding *bosco*. It's one of those delicious guest-less nights where the staff have long gone and I can regress gently into memories of my life and this big old house.

And, oh, how I have been treasuring this buried memory that has been unearthed by Mama Gidjane!

In my mind I can smell camphor in the breeze, I can hear the comforting sounds of pots and pans clattering in a kitchen, and the sweet strains of classical music on a gramophone ... I'm about ten years old, sitting on the bed in my grandmother's room. The bedcover has a floral pattern, with roses in peaches and pinks interlinked with veined green leaves. Excluding the dogs, cats, chickens, frogs, lizards, mice, hedgehogs and other creatures, it is just the two of us in the old house tonight. My parents have gone camping in Moçambique. Steven and Brett are away somewhere with friends. I like it like this.

Earlier on, we walked through the vegetable garden to collect things for dinner. 'How beautifully everything grows in the red Agatha soil,' said my grandmother, joy in her voice, if not a dash of amazement, since everything really does grow very well here indeed. The fennel and dill are plump, with a strong liquorice smell and big flat-topped yellow flowers like something out of a science fiction movie. There are rosemary bushes with their needles that taste like soap, parsley for cleansing the breath, nasturtiums for cleansing the lungs, mint for the love of it. There are frilly watery lettuces, glossy ribbed spinach leaves, tomatoes, small, medium, enormous; red peppers, chilies, sweet and tart gooseberries.

The skies rumble and get heavier, we eat omelettes in the kitchen next to the old Aga stove, omelettes made with fresh eggs and cheese and herbs and cherry tomatoes. The dogs lick the plates off, the cats drink milk off the table. The ginger one purrs and sits on my lap. I get sleepy and my granny leads me to her bedroom with a cup of very sweet tea with condensed milk as the wind whips the curtains and the rain begins its comforting splatter on the old tin roof. Underneath the rosy bedcover the bed is a delicious fug of smells. My grandmother's perfume, dogs, flowers, lavender. I snuggle under and in the distance I hear a rumble of thunder. My grandmother goes back to the kitchen and then suddenly there is a flash of lightning and the electricity trips.

'Cooeee, I'll get some matches,' she calls out, typically unfazed by power cuts and storms.

It is pitch dark. The wind is getting more frantic. I can hear the curtains flapping furiously and lie still, waiting for Ess to bring a lamp. The door is open and as my eyes get used to the dark I can make out the lawns above the pool, and the shapes of the fever tree leaves big and wild, like the flapping ears of night creatures.

My granny comes into the room with a paraffin lamp which she sets next to the bed, and a couple of candles, which she lights and places in holders around the room. 'Oh, listen to the thunder,' she says. She sounds happy, as if it were created especially for her. 'Thunder is a marvellous combination of the workings of hot rocks, cool winds, thermals and condensation,' she explains. 'Oh Bridgie, think of the wonder and the mystery of it all.' She sits on the edge of the bed and holds my hand.

The curtains are whipping the door, the lightning is getting closer and the thunder is crashing about. A sharp gust of wind flies in and the paraffin lamp crashes to the floor. There is a click in the air, like slender metal knitting needles being smacked together, then a burning smell and then the candles all go out at once as if a collective breath has been drawn. The door flies open and a giant flame, an almighty ball of fire, rolls into the room, licks up against the wall, sets the curtain alight and then disappears like a golden snake, a snorting mythical dragon, right out the door again.

A heavy pall of rain starts drumming against the glass.

'Bridgie,' cries my grandmother. Her voice sounds like the moon-light. 'Oh Bridgie,' she says, 'we have been visited by the fire gods. Let's have a stiff brandy and celebrate.'

'I want to make a garden, Granny,' I say, shocked and excited ...

Oh, how I have been treasuring this buried memory that has been unearthed by Mama Gidjane! It has sparked within me a desire to remember more about myself, instead of blotting it all out. And of course it has sparked an intense desire to go gardening.

I bury myself in my father's armchair in the study overlooking the mountains that change every day, and begin an uncertain journey into the world of shrubs and wild flowers, Zen gardens, cottage gardens, formal gardens, Renaissance gardens, Italian monastery gardens and collectors' gardens. I read about beds and borders, hedges and water features, about shade lovers, pot lovers, sun seekers and fast growers. I roll the names around on my tongue: lobelia, lily of the valley, larkspur, lady's slipper.

And when I look outside the study window, I look out on to a garden that changes with the seasons and the mountains that change every day. They are smiling old men, wrinkled elephants, knuckles on a fist, noses, thighs, crocodiles, prehistoric beasts inching towards us. A new bust was erected recently for my second cousin Delia who died of breast cancer, morphine-muddled and pain-riddled. When she died the garden cried. The leaves of the trees dripped tears, the winds moaned and shadows fell. The southern bou-bou wailed its mournful song, and then a shaft of buttery sunlight lit up the dead tree as if to suggest it was time to gather on the stoep to drink champagne and set Delia's spirit free.

The tree is home to owls, raptors, ravens and crows, to hadedas, long-crested eagles, buzzards and kites. When Benjamin was born, a flock of storks were blown off course and into the gardens on a strange yellow-coloured storm and the Dead Tree turned green, like a fever tree. Again, we rushed to the stoep to drink champagne and watch the puzzled, agitated storks as we took excited calls from the hospital.

When I got married an eagle owl flew into the tree at dusk, just as the ceremony was over and everyone was charging their glasses. When I got divorced it hailed and the tree dropped a huge branch on to the stone wall. Births, deaths, marriages and love affairs are sewn into this landscape, they are part of the trees, the soil, the birds and the flowers. They are what make this garden grow.

In summer, jacarandas, coral trees and flamboyants dance together in the greenery, and the mist and the mountains play hide and seek. The concrete statues take on a sombre air, as if they are statesmen or dignitaries observing a solemn parade, and the Brazilian kapok

149

showers the driveway with pink petals after the night's storm. In March, the pink tibouchinas drop their flowers and the cassia starts emerging, the colour of joy and daffodils. In autumn the purple penstemon starts to bloom, as the wild grasses become pale and bleached, and by winter the bougainvillea and poinsettia tangle in heady combinations of marmalades, crimsons and fiery reds. Throughout the year, a series of fountains and water features provide a soothing elemental mantra: *water over rocks, water over rocks.*

The guests come and go gently and easily, and no one is unmoved by the drama of the view and the loveliness of the garden. There is a marriage proposal – and acceptance – beneath the Dead Tree, and a romantic picnic for two alongside the Bibigar. We dispatch young lovers with blankets and baskets into the garden, and they re-emerge in the dark, looking rumpled and happy. One of the overnight parties is a couple who met here on a working trip and began a heady love affair. They were both married to other partners at the time, and Kings Walden and this garden was the setting for their four years of stolen happiness. And then they decided one night, sitting on the edge of the lawn watching the lights come on in the Lowveld below, that it was time for them to leave their partners and marry each other. They always book the same room.

One Saturday afternoon a wedding party arrives to have their photographs taken in the garden. It is a crowd of about fifty people, who are dressed up like they are in a ballroom movie. The bride is a picture of peach silk and chiffon, with taffeta and bling and golden powder on her beautiful black cheeks. The groom is impeccable in a black suit with a pink shirt, a slender cerise tie and pointed snakeskin shoes. There are strings of child bridesmaids in matching silk with Alice bands and lacy socks, clutching enormous sprays of roses in pinks and peaches. The guests are immaculate, in a stylish fusion of traditional meets modern, Africa meets Paris, urban meets rural.

The party assembles on the lawn in front of the Dead Tree, with the mountains as a backdrop. The afternoon light is golden, the mountains blue, and the sky above a bruised purple. The photographer patiently arranges everybody to suit his composition, pushing a little bridesmaid here, moving a grandmother there. He shoots a series of photographs in different poses – standing, sitting, formal, relaxed – and one with the groom holding the bride in his arms, as if he had just saved her from fainting.

And just as the last photograph has been snapped, a sunbeam shines down on the Dead Tree and it starts raining. It's a monkey's wedding – a sign of immense good luck – and the party breaks out in joy and laughter, and the old women start ululating and singing, the children run around giggling and chortling. The whole wedding is bathed in gold and joy and sparkly raindrops, as if the ancestors have decided to bless this particular party for no other apparent reason than the sheer delight of the spectacle.

It is wonderful to watch a garden move the souls of people, to see the stirring of beauty and happiness, and in the course of the next few days, out of my blackness and sorrow, a tiny frond begins to unfurl and I experience an almost forgotten emotion for the first time in three years.

Oh, how sweet that first surge of hope.

How sweet to feel, no matter how muted, that first impulse of reconnection with life on earth, to awake of a morning without black dread, to savour the very first sense of possibility in years that there is still love and joy, that there is still hope and that perhaps, just perhaps, there will always be hope because it is part of human nature, our intrinsic human tenacity.

Like a garden, hope begins with a single seed. And looking at the garden around me I remember that it, too, began with nothing but a patch of ground. In the beginning, this was just wilderness: 'We were surrounded by an immeasurable abyss of darkness and splendour. We built our empires on a pellet of dust revolving round a ball of fire in unfathomable space. Life, that Sphinx, with the human face and the body of a brute, asked us new riddles every hour.'[7]

In the beginning, here at Kings Walden, there was a 'dreadful fucking mess, frankly', as my mother says. The old farmhouse and garden had fallen into disrepair since my grandmother had grown too old to maintain such a big place and had moved up to Hunters Moon, to Brett's house. The roof had collapsed, swallows nested under the eaves, wild cats inhabited the bedrooms, damp and rain and moss and sun had created a micro-climate in the house where moss, lichen and ferns flourished.

Restoration began way back in 1986 and today Tana's garden is an entire philosophy, a lively allegory, a marvellous mix of tragedy and love. Like her mother had done before her, my mother gardened boldly in the face of adversity, commemorating life's events through plants and trees, flowers and shrubs, lions and gargoyles. Every time there was a crisis – and there were many – she made another bed, created another garden, built another courtyard.

'Raise high the roof beam, carpenters!' was her clarion call when the builders first began work on restoring the old Kings Walden farmhouse. This was in response to my Unfortunate Incarceration, as it is known in the family, at the whim of the apartheid government during the State of Emergency in 1986. For three long months I sat in an Eastern Cape prison as my demented mother ordered Victor the builder to keep raising the ceilings as a result of the claustrophobia she imagined I was experiencing.

Staccato images of hideous brutality came out of the first hearing of the Truth Commission in East London: disappearances and murders, the Cradock Four, the PEBCO Three; poisonings, assassinations, deaths in detention. The nature of the beast that had gripped the

---

[7] From Alfred Noyes, *The Unknown God.*

country in the eighties was panicky, repressive. Massive popular resistance to apartheid was met with rubber bullets, tear gas, buckshot, police roadblocks, spotlights, curfew, military forces in townships and media curbs. A week before I was detained, a friend was pulled out of his car at a police roadblock for wearing a badge that said: Zebras against Apartheid.

I was involved in the End Conscription Campaign (ECC) that kicked particularly sensitive political butt. The military focus had shifted from the borders to the townships and for the first time young white men and their families were questioning the value of their stake in maintaining apartheid. Alarmed at the cracks appearing in the white support base, the state struck out at Instigators and there went mother's little threat to law and order.

I was having a cup of tea at work when two security policemen appeared at my desk at *Grocott's Mail* on 3 July 1986 waving a detention order. From Grahamstown I was taken to Alexandria, a small coastal hamlet. I spent my first three days there without a change of clothing or toiletries, but was given food from the local hotel, such were the anomalies of being a white detainee.

I was then taken to North End Prison in Port Elizabeth, and after two weeks my detention order was extended to Indefinite, as it was called, at the behest of Law and Order Minister Louis le Grange. I was then transferred to Fort Glamorgan Prison in East London, about 120 kilometres up the coast. Ten years after it happened I went back to the prison, and there was a large banner hanging outside the gate that read *Warders for Peace*, using the same logo that we at ECC had used. The white dove symbol. The first time I came here, however, I was bundled out of a security police car, fingerprinted, made to strip naked, bend over, get dressed again and then led off to my cell.

The cell was very small. I could stand with outstretched arms and almost touch the walls on either side. There was a single metal bed that occupied the entire length of the cell. Above it, two narrow vertical windows looked on to a facebrick wall and a rectangle of sky. On the left of the bed there was a wooden dresser, toilet and basin. Above the foot of the bed a small window looked on to the passage and below it was a Listening Box attached to the wall, basically a one-way intercom that allowed warders to listen in to the cell. When I was first locked in here I simply shrank into the size. By the time I left I was like a surrealist painting where matchboxes and combs are the same size as people.

I spent almost a month in solitary confinement in this cell, locked in with a Bible, let out twice a day for half an hour to walk around a bare courtyard. Initially the isolation was strangely restful and then it became increasingly difficult to focus my thoughts or summon emotions. Moods weakened into a dull hum. My brain felt woolly, I kept shaking my head. My dreams were filled with people and greenery. I eventually stopped reading the Bible and simple lay there pitting myself against time. I had no idea when I would get out and time became a steady indistinguishable stream. No short cuts, no detours, just hours and minutes and seconds of time like a silent loop tape. I could hear the sea outside, the traffic, gossiping mynah birds. I could hear the mournful blasts of ship's horns, and on Sundays, the sad sweet sounds of the prison choir.

Eventually I was allowed to see the other detainees – two friends from Grahamstown – and we were locked up together in an *eetsaal* during the day, and allowed to knit, read and write letters. These 'privileges' were brokered by Spyker van Wyk, a notorious East London security policeman who got his nickname from nailing people's hands to the desk during interrogation.

As the winter in Agatha gave way to a blustery early spring, the ceilings got higher and higher and my mother's garden bolder and grander. She razed the ruins of the old tennis court and clubhouse to make way for the dam and the Bibigar, she graded the slopes in preparation for the signature acre of purple agapanthus. And she enlisted the help of Mama Gidjane to cast a spell upon the government and the security police.

Mama Gidjane set about performing daily detention-ending rituals on an article of my clothing. It was a black and yellow knitted dress in a beehive pattern, bought in a cheap Grahamstown store and designed for winter. It was hung up on an old tree in Lala's garden where it flapped about in the choppy winds, and Mama Gidjane sprinkled water on it and made incantations at sunrise and sunset. Herbs were gathered and sprinkled around the tree, branches were burnt and stones scattered.

One time Mama Gidjane 'got through' but she shook her head sadly and reported back that unfortunately the detainee was being uncooperative. Later her rituals became more frequent and my parents more desperate as every day, all day, the black and yellow dress continued to hang and flap from the tree in Lala's garden.

Then one day, ninety-three days after I was detained, it was a Friday, we were told *pak jou goed* and we were released into the world, clutching restraining orders forbidding us from attending gatherings of more than five people. We sat for four or five hours in silence, waiting to be collected by the police and taken back home. Where was home? The day we'd longed for had arrived and it was terrifying.

I caught a plane a few days later to Johannesburg – a midnight flight, packed with drunk army guys – and then my brothers drove me up to Kings Walden, up the Great North Road, past Warmbaths and Nylstroom, Naboomspruit, Potgietersrus, Pietersburg, Tzaneen, through towns where you could smell the fear and the hatred, past walls crawling with graffiti and resentment, past landscapes coloured in war and blood. It was October, the weather was snippy and gusty, dry and hazy. I was irritable, tetchy, brittle, confused and unable to perform the simplest task.

This was my first visit to the newly renovated Kings Walden, and when I arrived I went and lay under the Dead Tree and wept.

ॐ

As the country catapulted towards crisis, so Kings Walden's garden flourished and grew. After the rebuilding of the house was completed, my parents called in a *sangoma* to bless the house – and it was the same Dr Neverdie, who had come here as a younger man one Christmas when we were given pandas and who had told Steven he had a weak heart.

'How is your heart, *mfana*,' he asked Steven who was taking pictures and looking perky and relieved to have his sister back.

'*Lungile sharp*,' he replied, '*awudzi*'. (OK, sharp, good.)

We gathered on the stoep overlooking the mountains that change every day. My parents, Steven, Brett and my grandmother Ess. Melea and Mama Gidjane were there too of course, and welcomed Dr Neverdie as he arrived through the gates in the freshly painted white walls. He was older, plumper and more wrinkled, and when he laughed his chest wheezed like a pair of ageing bellows. His dress was less traditional – he wore jeans and a Tarzan leopard-print vest, with a cloth wrapped around his waist, sandals made out of tyre retreads, and a large pair of sunglasses.

This time Dr Neverdie had brought his python with him, its name was Mr Sharp, and he clung to it protectively and assured us it couldn't move very far or very fast at all. Its spirit however, was very strong, and it was a powerful blessing. And this time round Dr Neverdie didn't perform his ceremony with as much gusto as I remember from that Christmas Day in 1969. He wandered around the gardens, slowly, with Mr Sharp in his arms. It was good to be out, he sighed. Work was tough, there were a lot of problems in the community, people were being hassled by the cops, they were being jailed and beaten and their houses were being burnt down. Everyone was looking for protection and certainty and, frankly, well, he was just getting too old and tired to cope with it all. He adjusted his python, wiped the sweat off his brow with a soiled old hanky and accepted Melea's offering of a cold beer with distinct relief.

One of the great characteristics of the Hilton-Barbers is our ability to party on in the face of adversity and despite – or even because of – the ghastly political backdrop I recall the first few years after my parents moved back to the ancestral home as some of the jolliest and happiest in our lives – especially over Christmas and New Year. Tables groaned with food and alcohol, guests groaned with food and alcohol. My grandmother Ess, by now mad as a hatter, was accompanied everywhere by a vicious little terrier called Darling, and entertained us with tales of a nasty imposter who was pretending to be my father. We encouraged her to shout at him and Darling to chase him around a bit, just for the fun of it.

Tana made hams and turkeys and chickens. Once she even did a stuffed chicken inside a turkey. Inside the chicken, she said, was a stuffed mouse for the cats. She prepared farm-grown litchis in tequila, which were kept for a year in a dark cupboard and had a very similar effect to being shot in the stomach. She made quiches and pastas and roulades and pâtés, and Christmas puddings that dripped with brandy. It was a tradition that a few coins and my mother's wedding ring were baked into the pudding, and there was always an anxious moment or two when the pudding had been eaten and nobody had found the wedding ring.

'What if it's been swallowed?' Steven asked, and just as my mother's eyes widened in horror, he produced the wedding ring from behind his ear with a smile.

The wine flowed like the Letsitele River and family and friends fell happily about, the gardens outside grew and grew. Kings Walden's particularly decadent brand of hospitality became renowned. Guests brought wine and left with avocados and great bunches of basil; friends donated plants, statues, seeds, and even peacocks, which unfortunately had their throats slit by a slender mongoose the night they arrived. Tana began framing old family pictures to hang in the ancestral dining room.

'You never know what's inside,' said my parents excitedly one morning.

'Inside what?'

In his restoration work, the builder had unearthed my grandfather Billo's old safe, and my parents had called in a locksmith to come and open it in the hope that it contained money, gold bars, valuable shares, priceless antiques, or all of the above.

We gathered at a generous 11.30am to drink champagne and await the arrival of the locksmith. My mad grandmother was most concerned that someone was arriving and began to disappear into her military world, which was a combination of a siege mentality, gleaned largely from the propaganda that was on the radio which was on all the time, and a wild imagination.

'Magnus says we ought to be prepared,' she began. Magnus was of course Magnus Malan, then Minister of Defence who, in her mind, was not just English, but a close friend. She was actually one of his advisers, and the mention of Magnus's name usually involved the start of a difficult skirmish, since she would then want to lock the doors, shoot the servants and commandeer someone's car.

It was almost 2pm and practically everyone was drunk, including Ess who was merrily slugging back eggnogs, when the locksmith called to say he was going to be delayed. He had to make an emergency trip to Mbabane in Swaziland because the Bank of Swaziland had locked one of their vaults and couldn't open it again and the weekend was approaching and they had no money for the people.

He arrived a few days later, pleased to report that he had liberated the Swazi bank's money, and the family once again gathered, with champagne, to watch the opening of the safe and hopefully live happily and wealthily ever after. This time we had cunningly got Melea to take Ess for a walk in the garden so she wouldn't see the locksmith, his worker or his vehicle.

My father ushered us into the room where the safe was built into the wall. The locksmith took out his bag of tricks, inspected the lock, kicked the safe, and then barked out a series of instructions to his worker who immediately got busy doing all the real work. There was a great deal of fiddling and poking around the lock with different bits and pieces. The second bottle of champagne was dangerously low, and we were all getting a little bored when suddenly the safe door flew open, and the locksmith fell from his haunches on to his bottom.

We rushed forward and peered into the dim reaches of my grand-father's safe. Inside there lay, in a chiaroscuro light, an ageing packet of morphine and a silver syringe.

After an uncharacteristic family silence, Steven said loudly: 'Hey, I wonder if we can still use the morphine?'

'More champagne,' cried my mother, 'and a beer for the locksmiths. And pass the syringe, won't you, darling, it should hang as an ornament on some wall or the other, don't you think?'

But I think we were all secretly disappointed that there were no notes, gold bars, valuable shares, priceless antiques, or all of the above. We drank quietly and when the locksmith finished his beer, he wiped his hand across his cropped little moustache and stepped outside. My father saw him out to his car, and we heard Darling Dog barking and a loud 'Oh, for goodness sake!' as he realised that my grandmother was behind the wheel of the locksmith's car. Melea was trying to comfort the locksmith's terrified worker who was rubbing a bump on his head and sporting a torn trouser leg.

The first surges of hope and the stirrings of memories inspire me to spend time in Kings Walden gardens talking to my ancestors. I visit the burial sites of all our old family pets: Zingwe the Labrador, Darling Dog, Maselu the Burmese Cat; Mac, a sweet Labrador cross. My mother's favourite was a bad-tempered and beautiful Siamese called Fenje, who has a whole pavilion dedicated to her. One night I decide to drink champagne with Lala and slink off to the moonlight and shadows in the top garden, where there is an old concrete table. I set the paraffin lamps out, and a white table cloth and a vase of blue agapanthus. On a whim I take a handful of dog biscuits and scatter them into the evening to appease and acknowledge the spirit of Henry the terrier.

I find a box full of Chinese prayer papers and write messages on them and set them afloat in the Bibigar for all the 'women spirits' who have lived and worked and visited here. My grandmother, Melea, Mama Gidjane, my mother Tana, my girlfriends ... I set a scattering of rose petals afloat on the waters of the Elsie Tooley Memorial Fountain below the Dead Tree, a silver grey pond with a spitting heron. It used to be a little thatched rondavel, a terrifying place in which to spend the night as a child, inevitably ending in tears in my parents' room at 3am.

I wander down to the pool, taking a moment at the top of the steps leading down to the Bibigar. This is where my brother Brett and I shook hands on the 70th Birthday Agreement, which basically sets down that if one of us doesn't want to sell, he or she has veto. This was on my father's 70th birthday and part of a painful coming to terms with the fact that there were only two of us children left.

Halfway down, the steps that lead through the agapanthus to the Bibigar are intersected by Sarah's Fountain, a three-tiered fountain that drips water endlessly down into a low pool which is guarded by four lions. Around the fountain is pennyroyal and mondo grass. Sarah Cullinan was Brett's girlfriend who died in a car accident in Agatha in 1988. When she died, a flock of a hundred-odd ravens came down from the mountains to add their tragic Gothic signature to the dead tree's bone white fingers. She was twenty-eight years old and it changed everything I knew and felt about life, it was the first really sad experience that made me realise that things don't always turn out like they should.

I came back from London to spend time with Brett at Hunters Moon, where they had been living. We arrived as the sun was going down, poured ourselves wine and sat sadly and silently on the stoep, looking out at the magnolia and *mnali* tree, looking at the flowering camel foot bauhinia whose pale pink flowers dropped to the ground like tears. As the night cooled, the air filled with the scent of pennyroyal, and all the houseplants that grew and hung and decorated the stoep seemed to huddle closer, like friends: the hens and chickens, the money plants, wandering Jews, asparagus ferns and sword ferns. As it got dark enough for the tiny fruit bats to start flitting, a bushbuck wandered on to the lawn.

I spend an afternoon in the Italian Garden, which has an Italian-style axial design – it is a long rectangular bed of roses and mint and sorrel set into brick. At either end is an archway with a mirror, in front of which is a Roman bust. These busts represent my father David and his brother Guy – and reflect endlessly in a series of heads and roses whose effect is both elegant and witty. The monkeys love to sit on top of these busts, dirtying them and resulting in the rather silly impression that my father and his brother are wearing brown toupees like second-hand car salesmen.

The Italian Garden is dedicated to my father's side of the family, who may be Italian in spirit but actually come from Zimbabwe. To the right of the monkey-muddied busts is a small path that leads through more roses and azaleas to a tiled concrete bench that is decorated with angels and dedicated to my grandmother Mary. She was married to Harold, my father's father. Mary's garden is my garden *segreto*. It is the most undetectable and quietest place in the whole of Kings Walden. I come here when I want to smoke a joint, have a private moment or simply disappear.

A lady of great gentleness and dignity, says the plaque on the bench, and I can picture dear Mary doing crosswords, with her swollen legs bandaged and her big owl-like glasses. She was large and smelled of powder and soap. She married my grandfather twice. The second time was after the death of Alice, Harold's second wife, whom neither Steven nor I liked, and we sniggered cruelly over the fact that her little finger was permanently bent as a result of a severe parrot bite.

Mary's bench is surrounded by iceberg roses, white azaleas and camellias. There is moss on the brickwork, and another garden mirror alongside her bench that is covered with a rose-clad trellis and reflects the poetic tangle of roses and creepers and memories. They lived in Filabusi in Southern Rhodesia, a harsh, dry cattle ranch surrounded by bush and wilderness. My grandfather was eventually killed in an ambush; Mary survived.

It was here in the Italian garden that the ancestors spoke to me way back in 2000. It was a blisteringly hot day and I had disappeared into my garden *segreto* to escape from the pain and suffering inside the house. The cats lay panting on the couches. My mother Tana had taken to drinking heavily and firing random shots into the ceiling in the bedroom, and my father and the dogs were most disturbed. The farm was in danger of being taken by the Land Bank because of its enormous debt – and their lives were on a knife edge.

I sat on Mary's bench and watched the monkeys playing in the *mitserie* trees and the power line poles at the end of the Italian Garden. Using their long tails as rudders, they scurried across the power lines and leapt about the poles like gymnasts. One monkey stopped for a break and sat on top of the pole. He was scratching around and grasped one of the transformers in his hand. He looked around, and then grabbed hold of the other transformer and I watched in horror as the monkey exploded with a bang. The air filled with smoke and the smell of electricity and burnt flesh.

'Oh fuck,' I thought to myself. 'There goes the farm.'

I wake up and watch a blood red sunrise. And wander down to

spend an hour or two watching the first rays of sun warm the mountains and bathe Steven and Benjamin and Andrew's garden in sunlight. It is such a gentle morning, and I feel, for the first time, able to sit alone here without wanting to cry, without wanting to die. The white camellias and iceberg roses are flowering, and underneath them the baby's breath and zebra grasses catch the warming sun. For the first time I think of smiles and curls instead of dead feet and dead blue faces. When I picture Steven's face I can hear him talking, see the way his shirt fell, the warmth in his voice. I think of Benjamin as a tiny starburst that temporarily saved me from Steven's death, and of Andrew's lovely mouth. Perhaps if I change my notion of death, I think, it will change my notion of joy.

Chapter fourteen

It was full moon the night my grandfather Billo died.

The garden was awash with lemon moonlight. The giant syringa tree cast its enormous charcoal shadow across the lawns and the owls hooted. A ginger cat stalked a lizard at the foot of a creeper-clad pot. He's not going to wake up, thought my grandmother Ess, when she saw the moon sail into the sky above the Lowveld. And then I am going to be a widow and everything will be different for ever and ever.

Billo was pathetically thin and pale, sleeping under a cotton blanket in the early evening. Melea was in the kitchen, everything was clean and tidy and ready for dinner. My grandmother was drinking whisky, and rose every now and again from her chair on the stoep to check on my grandfather.

The garden was lit like a stage set, with paraffin lamps and candles. Billo's Fountain, a spitting lion, was trickling calmly and the night was warm but not muggy. My grandmother and Melea had spent ages filling a series of lamps and carried them across the lawn and placed them in an arch beneath Billo's Fountain, so that the water shimmered and shone and it seemed like the lion was spitting golden water. And the moon sailed steadily into the sky, turning as orange as fire as it passed through the dust of the Lowveld, and then yellowing and flying into the sky, like a queen, casting her serene colours over the hot bush, the subtropics and the mountains.

It must have been about ten o'clock when Melea came out to the stoep and stood a moment in the full moon light alongside my grandmother who was sitting on a chair now, a half empty bottle of whisky at her side.

Melea put her hand on Ess's shoulder. 'He's gone,' she said. And then walked back inside the house. My grandmother got up, took a great swig from the bottle and disappeared into the garden. Her immediate and overwhelming sensation was one of relief, but she felt shocked and frightened. She walked up a grassy path into the top garden, where red salvia danced with yellow daisies under the moonlight. She sat in the cool moonlit night and quietly finished the bottle of whisky as the new day broke.

'Some bodies are difficult to dress,' said Melea to Mama Gidjane, 'and some bodies are easy to dress. She had washed Billo and was preparing to dress him for the funeral. 'This old *mokgekolo* here, he is easy to dress. Oh, and he was such a good and handsome man.' She looked at his body, dressed in a white cotton shirt, with a handkerchief tucked sartorially into the pocket.

'The hardest one to dress was his first wife,' said Melea, a smile crossing her face.

Mama Gidjane shot her a quizzical look.

'She had been sleeping with a man in the army,' said Melea, doing a suggestive wiggle of the hips, 'and had a heart attack in the middle of it …'

Mama Gidjane started to giggle

'I had to rearrange her,' chuckled Melea, 'to look like a good and proper wife.'

'Jona jo,' cackled Mama Gidjane. *'Jona jo.'*

My grand-uncle Popsa found my grandmother Ess the next morning, fast asleep in the top garden with her head under a yellow daisy bush. He took her in his arms and held her as she woke, and as her eyes opened, he seized her face in his hands and gave her a passionate kiss.

'I am so sorry you are a widow, Mrs Tooley,' he said, gruffly, and then he took her by the hand and led her down the grassy path and into the kitchen.

At Billo's funeral my grandmother Ess read from Homer's *Iliad*:

O fortunate old man! Whose farm remains
For you sufficient, and requites your pains;
Though rushes overspread the neighbouring plains,
Though here the marshy grounds approach your fields,
And there the soil a stony harvest yields.
Your teeming ewes shall no strange meadows try,
Nor fear a rot from tainted company.
Behold! Yon bordering fence of sallow-trees
Is fraught with flowers; the flowers are fraught with bees:
The busy bees with a soft murmuring strain,
Invite to gentle sleep the labouring swain
While from the neighbour's rock, with rural songs,
The pruner's voice the pleasing dream prolongs,
Stock doves and turtles tell their amorous pain,
And, from the lofty elms, of love complain.

Not long afterwards her sister Lala came to stay. 'I'll help you go through his things and we can tidy them up and sort them out and everyone will feel better,' said Lala practically. She arrived with her usual flourish of hatboxes, music books, make-up bags and bottles of everything from perfume to absinthe. She had a fake fox fur and several different wigs.

'We are going to have a week of drinking, laughing, gambling and playing the piano,' said my grandmother Ess to her sister, 'to mourn my departed husband and lover.'

'A wake!' cried Lala. 'What an excellent idea.'

She walked into the lounge, opened the piano and began playing *Roll out the Barrel* in a jazzy honky-tonk style.

'Ess, my dear,' she said, 'let's have a bottle of Billo's finest wine.'

As the heat of the day eased, Ess and Lala went and sat at the view and drank cocktails, and Ess told her about her broken heart and her relief and her loneliness and her new gardening plans. Lala drank and listened, and then she told Ess about her boring husband and her affair and her loneliness and her music and how she still longed for Henry's warm little body. And the doves cooed and the loeries cackled and the mountains got darker and, in the distance, little lights began to twinkle, like shrimp boats arriving in a night-time harbour.

'Let's put on our very best gowns and play the piano and dance in the lounge,' said Lala. And so the sisters dressed up in their finest dresses, with boas and hats and cigarette holders and jewellery and wigs and far too much perfume. Lala played the piano and Ess sang and they threw their glasses into the fire – 'we have to have one even though it isn't really cold' – and pretended to be wild Spanish trollops in a hacienda, whose feet just wouldn't stop dancing.

'Yariba yariba, yariba,' Lala shouted as her fingers flew up and down the keyboard. She was playing standing up and shimmied and shook and swung her hips, and sweat poured down her temples.

'Hasta manyana,' yelled my grandmother Ess and flung another glass into the fire.

The moon slipped down the other side of the sky and Orion's Belt was low in the west. Dawn was only an hour or two away. The sisters wandered into the garden with blankets and more cognacs and went and lay down under the stars on the lawns and woke up the next morning, shaded by the syringa tree, with terrible hangovers.

For the next twenty-odd years, my grandmother Ess lived alone at Kings Walden, hosting parties and gatherings, luncheons and celebrations. She adored her animals and her garden, and thought often and fondly of her husband. She leased the farm to a manager whom she hounded with unrelenting ferocity and walked for miles and miles every day over the farmlands. And she gardened with passion and zeal.

Under her gifted planter's hands, Kings Walden's garden grew lustily. She planted forest fever trees, cassias, lasiandra, tibouchina and camel's foot. She planted agapanthus, acanthus, clivia, impatiens. She planted great orange aloes, red poinsettias, golden honeysuckle and creamy jasmine.

She planted great banks of shrubs and colour, experimenting with the unity between garden and countryside, exploring garden naturalism. She loved water features, creating ponds and pools around benches and statues, many of which are still here, their forms less sharp, a toe missing here, an ear broken there. 'The 18th century English landscape garden,' wrote English gardener, Penelope Hobhouse, 'was England's greatest contribution to western civilization. Its implications were immense. It represented a whole philosophy, intimately connected with literature and painting, often allegorical in meaning and classical in derivation.'[8] My grandmother wholeheartedly agreed.

---

[8] Penelope Hobhouse, *Garden Style*.

We visited often, visits that are etched in my mind like an image from an old-fashioned biscuit tin: two boys and a girl and a dog running through a green meadow of happiness. And then one day we were amazed to see that our grandmother's hair had turned completely white overnight. 'Hello there,' she said, when she opened her bedroom door, 'so pleased to see you all. Magnus and I have been waiting ...'

Chapter fifteen

The first sign of spring in Agatha is the flowering of the coral trees. The coral trees attract sunbirds and weavers and seed eaters and their branches become a thickly twittering fest. The coral trees are visible everywhere, peeking out of plantations, standing out of green valleys. Long ago, their first burst of bright red flowers served as a warning sign to the early settlers in the Lowveld that summer was approaching and with it, too, malaria. It was time to head for higher ground.

'Shortly before the green haze of leaflets appears,' I read in a tree book, 'dark shoots with furry knobs thrust out in all directions from the branches – singly and in bunches. These soon lengthen and the knobs swell. Their bases take on a scarlet glow and the tree is soon decked with masses of red-hot "soldering irons". These in turn, develop into long triangular heads of beautiful, scarlet, locust-shaped flowers.'[9] I am beginning to appreciate the joy of trees, plants and flowers again.

---

[9] Cythna Letty, *Trees of South Africa*.

And I am also starting to stretch out into my new space at Stone Cottage, like a cat. My bond is finally registered with the bank, setting me free of the awful Mr Schnitzel, and the money from the sale of my house in Joburg finally comes through. I upgrade from *dooswyn* to bottles, I buy new clothes. I go through boxes of photograph albums, and come across piles of letters and notebooks, diaries and memorabilia. I am amazed how young I look in photographs, how earnest and innocent.

My first day of high school: a big hat, slightly too big grey uniform, blonde hair. 1977, the year after the Uprisings, as we called them, when people's domestic workers didn't appear at work and the school windows were covered in diamond mesh, in case of bombs. There was chatter in the school corridors about who was going where. Most of my Jewish friends were set to emigrate – either to Israel, the US or Great Britain.

When I started high school Steven was a year ahead of me and Brett had already left. I still had the same problem with authority that had been fermenting in primary school, and it didn't take me long to start standing at the back of the queues, chirping up from the back of the class and rearranging my uniform to look rebellious.

We still lived in the big thatched house at 12 Northumberland Avenue, and I moved to a big bedroom that opened out on to the garden and was shaded by a wild pear tree that dropped its fruit in summer, creating great rotting piles that caused frequent slipping and lots of work for the long-suffering gardener.

My parents continued their Entertaining at every opportunity, and Brett's friends, young hairy students, were now part of the social milieu. My mother was extremely open-minded – she bought me my first bra, told me about contraception, that I shouldn't fall pregnant, and that I should sing loudly on approaching my brothers' outside cottage since their first girlfriends appeared. Whistle or sing, she said, and always knock.

My brothers' friends adored my parents. The house in Northumberland Avenue was the first place many saw a 'blue movie', as they were called, and tried alcohol and cigarettes and were encouraged to be adventurous and fun. Against a backdrop of wild boys and wild parents, my own explorations went unheeded. By the time I was fifteen I was practically delinquent. I had been caught shoplifting, had tried cigarettes, alcohol, dagga and cough mixture. By the time I was sixteen I had had sex, LSD and Mandrax, all of which seemed peculiarly normal suburban experiences, and usually took place at home or in the park across the road.

I dressed in Indian skirts and long flowing dresses, and sported bangles and bracelets on my wrists and ankles. I sewed handbags and waistcoats and went to pottery lessons and art classes. I immersed myself in a heady exploration of Woodstock, the punk movement, the beat poets, reggae, heavy metal and Ken Kesey's magic bus. I took with alarming ease and pleasure to anything that was against the system, anything naughty and rebellious. I hated school, the strictures, the stupidity. The headmaster was the incarnation of all evil although, thankfully, I had a brilliant English teacher in Standard Eight who encouraged my writing and probably prevented me from becoming a groupie or a total dropout. I was deeply sensitive and utterly brazen. I was caught bunking, I was caught smoking, I was kept late for being cheeky. I was never going to crack the school leadership system.

Towards the end of my matric year, a group of four friends and I broke into the prefects' room on a Saturday night and played spin the bottle and got drunk, which was still a novelty then. I ended up naked with the school flag wrapped around me and vomited over the balcony.

I'm not sure whether to laugh or cry at some of the memories in my photographs, and then one afternoon I decide on a whim to unpack one of Steven's old trunks of photographs instead, and flip through kaleidoscopic images of our lives in the eighties – rallies, demonstrations, burning car tyres, smoky townships, police in sunglasses, mothers weeping for their dead children – and our lives in the nineties, when Mandela was released and we realised that the winds of change were blowing our way, star-struck and drunk with a sense of history. There are photographs of family and friends, some dead, some alive, some long forgotten. I come across images of *sangomas* and healers and ceremonies showing people in trances drinking goat's blood and smearing their bodies with strange potions.

My brother Brett arrives to spend some time at his house, Hunters Moon. Hunters Moon is a green-roofed farmhouse that was built by my grandfather in the late forties. It is thick with benevolent spirits and memories. So many people – family, relatives, friends, farmers, locals – have stayed here; if the walls could talk, we'd probably all be in jail. Next to the house is an enormous *mnali* tree that my mother planted when Brett was born and, below it, a magnolia that marked my brother Steve's entrance into the world. They thought he had a rash when he came back from the Tzaneen Hospital, but it was just the lipstick kisses of all the nurses.

We sit on the stoep, the fire going at one end, drinking and talking and delighting in the fact that we are all gathered, like elephants, in the valley of our ancients. How lucky we are, we say to each other, that through all of it, through everything, we both have a sanctuary near the Mother Ship, near the garden of our ancestors. Our space is comfortable, thoughtful, warm. The evening is still and a big orange moon is sailing into the skies above the fire tower and we are swapping tales of this lovely house and its eccentric inhabitants. His eyes get that happy-times look.

One of the bravest things my brother Brett has done was live at Hunters Moon with my crazy grandmother and Darling Dog in the cottage. 'She is not going to an old age home,' said my mother firmly, despite the growing concern in the Agatha community as a result of my grandmother's activities. She had recently hitched into town and bought a car under false pretences. Darling Dog had fathered yet another litter of puppies at some or other compound, and she was overfeeding the Dexter cow that lived in the paddock below the house.

It had got so fat, said Brett, that it could barely move and yet my grandmother kept on feeding it, slipping into the paddock with bags of food and shouting at anyone who tried to prevent her from doing it. She was regarded with fear by the locals, which was exactly the right response, since my grandmother would think nothing of charging even the biggest Sotho with her walking stick and her ferocious Darling Dog. Eventually Brett sold the Dexter for handsome profit to a butcher in Nkowankowa and they had to try and get it on to the back of a bakkie in the middle of the night so as not to incur the wrath of Ess.

Sitting on the old stoep at Hunters Moon, Brett and I laugh and talk and drink wine.

Baap.

'Did you hear that?' I say to him.

We listen in silence.

Baap.

'That.'

'Frog?' he says, cocking his head.

Baap.

'There it is again.'

'I'd say frog,' he says, this time with more conviction. 'It's a good sign that rain is on the way.' As the author of several natural history books, he is the official voice of Nature and the Bush in the family.

Baap.

'Painted reed frog?' I venture.

'Could be,' he says.

'Haven't heard one of those in a while,' I sigh, connecting with nature.

We listen in silence.

Baap. Baap.

Then a small pebble lands on the floor of the stoep. We peer into the darkness. Another tiny pebble hits the balcony edge. Brett gets up, flicks on the torch and shines it out across the lawn and into the darkness.

There is Eric the gardener trying to get our attention from behind the electric fence: *'Baas,'* he's crying hoarsely, *'baas ...'*

Chapter sixteen

It was most mysterious indeed, everyone said, how the night that Elsie Margaret Tooley died a great big lightning bolt shot out of the sky and hit the ancient bluegum tree that stood at the edge of the lawns at Kings Walden. It was most mysterious, of course, because it was the middle of goddamn winter, the non-rainy season, and there wasn't even a flicker of a storm in the skies. But this giant bolt of lightning simply shot out of the sky in the middle of the night and zapped the bluegum tree and when everybody looked again in the morning, it was already bone white.

The day before my grandmother died I sat with her and my mother and Melea in the little cottage at Hunters Moon and we drank tea and champagne, and the three generations of women compared hands and feet and freckles and elbows.

'Look at that,' I said in amazement. On each of our right feet there was a big chocolate beauty spot in exactly the same place.

Steven came and took photographs of the three of us, and of Melea and Ess, Brett and Sara, and Darling Dog. All of us together and in interesting combinations, like Melea, Darling Dog and Ess. She was bedridden then, eighty-seven and just back from hospital.

She suffered a mild stroke while we were out. Someone had called an ambulance and she'd been taken to hospital. Tana went to fetch her, where she lay, pitifully, in dire agony, singing nursery rhymes. She was incontinent, she would never walk again, didn't know what was happening to her. Take me home, she cried.

Tana organised an ambulance to take her home that afternoon and sat with her in the back of it and she shrieked and yelped in pain as the ambulance bounced over the dirt road.

Back at Hunters Moon we settled her into her bed and she was so happy to be in her own home again. We put huge bunches of flowers around her bed, and brought in the freshly brushed Darling Dog. 'My pills,' begged Ess, and my mother handed her a small blue pill that we had been keeping on her instruction in the bathroom cupboard.

As the sun started slipping down the sky, Tana opened a bottle of champagne and poured them each a glass. They were alone in the cottage, mother and daughter. My grandmother swallowed her pill. Her physical pain went very quickly and she was so relieved to be at home. Her spirits were high and she was chatty, although she wasn't really making much sense. She talked about her husband and the farm and all the lovely things she had done. She talked about her garden and Darling Dog and then after a few glasses she became drowsy and fell asleep.

'I knew she was going to die,' said Tana, and she went outside into the night and flung Ess's champagne glass into the night, past the old concrete swimming pool choked with weeds and grass, past the yew row, into the wild, wild bush, the untamed *bosco*.

At about 10pm Ess slipped into a coma and, a little while later, she gave what doctors call the death rattle, a snoring noise from her throat. A few moments later, Melea said, taking Tana's hand, 'She's gone, *mammie,* she's gone.' And outside in the inky, wintry night, sparkling with yellow and pink stars and the tiniest wisp of cirrus clouds in the west, a great finger of lightning shot out the skies and shot through the bluegum tree that stands guard at the edge of the lawns at Kings Walden.

Chapter seventeen

The skies blacken, lightning starts flickering and thunder rumbles reassuringly in the distance. There's a build-up of clouds in the east, and the sound of the Burchell's coucal in the trees, like someone is pouring water into a ceramic pot. It won't be long before Stone Cottage will be blessed with the first spring rain, the first promise of summer.

Inspired by reading tales of the healing origins of gardening and the life-giving properties of herbs, I decide to make a herb garden. I imagine great scented rosemary bushes, bunches of basil filling the air, oreganum creeping happily along the ground, while thyme, fennel, dill, sorrel and tansy grow in a pottager style tangle. I imagine myself as an earth mother, dispensing farm-grown herbal remedies to my visiting friends for their everyday urban ailments.

I find a copy of a book called *Pippa's Organic Kitchen Garden*. On the cover is the plump and glowing Pippa wearing a decidedly untrendy blue checked shirt, black leggings and hiking boots. She is, however, holding a basket of the finest, glossiest most delicious looking Class-A fruit and veggies. Excitedly, I had read the blurb on the inside cover: Follow Pippa Greenwood create an organic kitchen garden from scratch, it said, and see how you too can grow fresh fruit, vegetables and herbs free from the dangers of chemicals and genetic modification ...

'Transforming a sloping patch of rough grassland into a kitchen garden was the start of a whole new adventure,' enthused Pippa in one of the chapters. I felt a great desire to be good like Pippa, and rushed off to the local nursery and bought a whole load of plump little seedlings.

It's a disaster.

After about two hours in the sun, despite a good watering by Golden Good, the gardener I have just taken on, the plump little seedlings are wilting and yellowing. Over the course of the next day or two, about half of them die off, the rest are plucked out by curious monkeys and the few remaining stragglers are showing signs of considerable strain.

I sit disconsolately down on a rock overlooking my desperate vegetable garden and nearly sit on a snake that slithers past, fat as a stocking, and disappears into a clump of ageing agapanthus.

I flee to the house.

'Pippa *se moer*,' I think nastily – and decide on a whim that I am going to go big and remove the entire avenue of water-sucking pine trees that has been irritating me so much with its brooding melancholy Alpinism.

I put the word out on the local network by telling Golden Good that I am looking for someone who will fell the pine trees and take the wood for nothing, *mahala*. I call one of my kindly relatives who kindly says she'll put the word out too.

'You bought seedlings from a nursery?' she exclaims in surprise when I tell her about my sorry gardening effort. 'And you planted them in the full sun at this time of year?'

Gardeners, they say, have no secrets. And so my relative tells me how I should rather buy seeds – much cheaper and more fun – and put them in trays and keep them warm and protected and snuggle them together to keep them moist and – for goodnesssakes! – if I needed plants, I should come to her and why don't I start with pots around the house ... And think of all the stock at Kings Walden.

And so it is that I begin my own garden.

They say it takes seven years to make an established garden, but they also say that once you start you can never stop. They say you should be patient and they say you shouldn't rush but the first time I sink my own hands into the red Agatha soil, it is as if I have put them into a socket. My fingers tingle, my elbows twitch, my hair curls ever so slightly and a smile spreads across my face as I feel the thrum of energy of another world whose essence contains the dust of millions of years of humankind.

I buy seed packets and seed trays and plant my herbs in pots and water them and keep them snug and moist and a few days later they begin emerging and unfolding and I feel like God. I begin to grow herbs for a kitchen patio garden – and when they start growing, I get bolder and start taking cuttings from other plants and slipping them.

Golden Good unpacks the storeroom and unearths rhino lashers, cutters, pangas and slashers. He attacks scruffy old azaleas like a ninja, slicing them down to branches and stumps. He hacks away at invaders, pulls out weeds, and pulls creepers out of the cracks.

I start by clearing the beds around the house and, as I clear, old marmalade bushes, neglected old hibiscuses and scraggly old lavenders emerge. I prune and clip and dig and clear and water. I throw seeds to the fields, to the wind, to the meadow, I fling mixed scatter packs.

I grow a loofah from a seed and plant it next to the outside shower. I plant impatiens and ageratum, lilies and ferns, filched from Kings Walden. I arrange for bags of lavender and catnip to be prepared, and spend most of my days and early evenings wandering round and round the house, clipping and snipping and planting. I cannot stop myself. I plant seeds for all the ancestors – for Melea and Fernandez, for my grandmother Ess, for Steven and Benjamin and Andrew. Like an anxious mother hen, I worry that the spring rain will be gentle on my babies.

Which of course it is, being spring rain. And I watch in amazement as tiny seeds push their curious green noses into the Agatha air and rise towards the sunlight.

And then one afternoon, a white bakkie comes trundling down the driveway at Stone Cottage. It stops outside the house and a young black guy gets out and looks back up the avenue of pine trees.

I go outside.

'*Le kae, mammie,*' he says, 'my name is Elvis.'

He is a pine tree feller, he tells me with a twinkle, and promises to take away the irritating avenue of pines and their brooding, melancholic Alpinism for ever. He will start tomorrow he says. And he disappears into the spring afternoon.

There are layers of life emerging everywhere in the garden. Praying mantises step carefully over leaves and branches, spiders weave their silver threads across impossible places, birds twitter, snakes slip into sunny spots, an extraordinary array of insects appears with their ancient prehistoric antlers and horns and thoraxes.

By the next morning, however, Elvis and his promised team of fellers have failed to arrive and I curse African time and decide to take a drive in the ageing Black Beauty. I head out up the driveway, and turn left on to the tar road that leads to the Agatha wilderness area. I head instinctively to the Forestry, as we call it, my mind imagining waterfalls and water thrumming over ancient rocks, enormous grandiflora trees and old figs and *waterbessies* and their coolth and calm.

I pass a series of cottages along the old dust road, one of which is blooming with spring delight. Purple and white azaleas, pink camellias and lilac and white yesterday-today-and-tomorrow bushes are grouped together in a show of colour, and the beds are mixed with lavender and tansy and yarrow and some heavenly purple flowers. There are day lilies and tiger lilies and Inca lilies and flame lilies. And there, just behind the gate, is a bed of sunflowers whose happy faces are turned towards the sun and they are beaming like a postcard.

I stop the car to have a look.

There is not much to beat a happy sunflower, I think, and, of course, being genetically predisposed, I decide to climb over the gate and take one, just to remind me of life and spring and the first surge of hope and possibility.

I climb on to the gate and halfway up I lean forward to grab the tallest sunflower I can get. As I grab hold of a beauty – oh, you are going to be mine, I think greedily – the cottage door opens and a guy comes out.

I have been bust.

He stands there for a moment, hands on hips and then he says: 'Shall I get you a pair of secateurs?'

I laugh.

'I saw it and just had to have it,' I say.

'It will be yours,' he replies. His eyes are like blue crystals and he has nice feet. He goes inside the house and comes out with a pair of garden secateurs and cuts the sunflower, and I climb over the gate and take it and say thank you. And then he says: 'When this is finished, let the seeds dry and scatter them in your garden and you can have a whole field. Would you like to see the rest of the place?'

And so we walk around the cottage and he shows me the old camellias and yesterday-today-and-tomorrow bushes and he tells me about the azaleas that were planted here by the early residents of Agatha, and about the ancient flame trees and flamboyants and figs that they planted, and how he found the pine trees irritating with their brooding melancholy Alpinism.

We discuss the pom-pom bushes that will be flowering soon, and the yellow arum lilies in the shade garden and the lovely spotted cowslips, elephant ears and delicious monsters and how nice it looks when the stones are covered with green moss and how good it feels underfoot.

And I leave hours later, when the sun is playing piano on the spines of the mountains that change every day, with my happy sunflower and a large packet of parrot food, which I have been advised to scatter. The rumps and folds of the mountains look green and plump and I can see sheets of water glistening on the ancient rocks.

I turn into the avenue and bump down towards my old Stone Cottage. When I get to the top of the drive, I look down and I see that Elvis has arrived and felled the first pine tree and it has landed on the roof of my house!

I don't know if there is a Sotho word for 'ball hair' but I imagine it was doing the rounds as I walked slowly down the drive, my eyes saucer-wide in disbelief. *Le kae mammie,* says Elvis with a sheepish grin, 'do you have a tape measure?'

And I notice Mama Gidjane laughing next to his white bakkie, laughing and cackling and clawing herself with delight.

Miraculously, the pine tree hasn't caused an ounce of damage. The soft part of the tree has simply given my roof a good brushing, and the tree is sliced up and rolled away and, along with the others, disappears some days later in an enormous truck – and the canvas is clean: tabula rasa.

Over the course of the next few weeks, the entire Agatha landscape is transformed with the spring rains and the slow wheel into summer. Azaleas, bursting into an array of pinks, peaches, apricots tinged with plum streaks. The tiboboya trees burst into yellow, the colour of rubber bath ducks and daffodils and happiness. The rain brings bursts of dragonflies that shed their wings in a state of frenzy and drive the cats completely wild with delight.

The clivias burst into oranges and peaches and the tree ferns' new buds unfurl, foetus-like. The sun reflects off the tiny pond in the middle of the Sunken Garden, and lights up silvery spider webs and drops of moisture. I stop and gaze at the Elsie Tooley Memorial Fountain, for my grandmother. It has in the centre a spitting heron, and foam nest frogs have started to make their home – it looks like shaving cream – under the heron's throat, giving it a rather silly appearance. Below, the roses are getting ready to bloom.

I wander round the garden of my ancestors, watching their spirits move in the buds and the blossoms, in the changing colours and the play of light. I think of our family and its tapestries and tragedies and tribulations, and I find, somehow, what I was hoping to find, and I quote:

I found, what I should have known all along, of course, that it was the present that was haunted, and that the past was not full of ghosts. The phantoms are what you carry around with you, in your head, like you carry dreams under your arm.

And when you revisit old scenes it is yourself as you were in the past, that you encounter, and if you are in love with yourself – as everybody should be in love with himself, since it is only in that way, as Christ pointed out, that a man can love his neighbour – then there is a sweet sadness in a meeting of this description. There is the gentle melancholy of the twilight, dark eyes in faces upturned in a trancelike pallor. And fragrances. And thoughts like soft rain falling on old tomb-stones.[10]

I wander home down the jacaranda-lined avenue past the little dam and the house where my grandmother stayed when she first came to Agatha. I wander along the banks of the dam where Steven and Brett and I used to practise driving Lala's car, and I stroll down to Stone Cottage where Melea and Fernandez shared their first naked and shivering kiss. I see the first sunflowers are starting to pop out of a bed near the tap, and a spider lily has started to flower outside my cottage, its spindly white arrangement so perfect, so outlandish. Next to it is a giant delicious monster and I see with delight that it has started to flower too. I gaze at the creamy white thing that is sliding out of a leafy green fold and it is so perfect and phallic and incredible that I reach for my cellphone and call the man with ice blue eyes and lovely feet.

'I'm coming round,' I say. 'I need some more advice on those sunflowers.'

---

[10] Herman Charles Bosman, *Bosman at his Best.*

Acknowledgements

Robert Ardrey, *The Hunting Hypothesis*. Collins, 1976

Herman Charles Bosman, *Bosman at his Best*. Human & Rousseau, 1965

Judith Chatfield, *The Classic Italian Garden*. Rizzoli International Publications, 1991

Louis Changuion (ed.) *Tzaneen 75 years*. Town Council of Tzaneen, 1994

Penelope Hobhouse, *Garden Style*. Winward Francis, 1988

Peter Joyce, *The Golden Escarpment*. Struik, 1986

Ronald King, *Great Gardens of the World*. Peerage, 1985

Cythna Letty, *Trees of South Africa*. Tafelberg, 1975

Alfred Noyes, *The Unknown God*. Sheed & Ward, London, 1934

B Wongtschowski, *Between Woodbush and Wolkberg: Googoo Thompson's Story*. B E H Wongtschowski, 1987

Copyright credits

Printed in Great Britain
by Amazon